HOW FAST CAN YOU SPOT THE EIGHT KEY WORDS IN THIS PARAGRAPH?

The Civil War was costly, so the federal government in Washington had to find a way to pay for it. Therefore, Congress adopted the first of a series of revenue laws in August 1861. Among them—our first income tax.

You can do it in a few seconds *if* you know the simple secrets of speed thinking and speed reading—the two elements that make *Super Reading* the real breakthrough book in teaching you to read, not just more quickly, but with dramatically increased comprehension. So why wait any longer? Become a rapid reader today!

SUPER READING

Key words: Washington, Congress adopted, August 1861, first income tax

Also by Learn, Inc.

SUPER VOCABULARY

Published by
WARNER BOOKS

SUPER READING

LEARN, INC.,

BY
Margaret Morgan Byrum

WARNER BOOKS

A Warner Communications Company

WARNER BOOKS EDITION

Warner Books, Inc.
666 Fifth Avenue
New York, N.Y. 10103

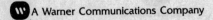 A Warner Communications Company

Printed in the United States of America

First Printing: August, 1988
10 9 8 7 6 5 4 3 2 1

Contents

Message from the Publisher

In both our personal and business lives, our ability to communicate with others is constantly being tested. Because of the continuous deluge of new information and knowledge generated by our technical world, we need to be able to process increasing amounts of information accurately and rapidly.

People who cannot receive precise messages are deprived of a way to measure and evaluate new ideas and information. The vast sums of money spent for word processing systems and computers to increase productivity are of use only if people can handle the information effectively. Information is of no value unless individuals can learn from it, make decisions, and take action.

Super Reading provides all the skills necessary for general communication tasks as well as for highly specialized needs. The entire sequence of skill development is comprehensive, mature, and relevant. It has been proven effective with hundreds of thousands of people; it's experience-based and results-oriented.

Use *Super Reading* as your springboard to success every time you need to read, think, and learn. If you apply yourself to this program, you will develop skills to use for a lifetime!

Good luck!

Bruce E. Corley

Bruce E. Corley
Publisher

SUPER READING

Learn, Inc.

Profile of Reading Habits

Are you an efficient reader? Take a few minutes to analyze your reading habits by completing this profile. Place an X in the column that describes your present reading habits.

When I Read	Always	Sometimes	Seldom
1. I change my rate of speed, depending on the type of material I read.			
2. I concentrate on what I'm reading and control my mind's wandering to other subjects.			

When I Read	Always	Sometimes	Seldom
3. I pay attention to the paragraphs and how they're organized.			
4. I use punctuation to help me understand what the writer means.			
5. I look over the entire article or book to find important parts that help me decide to read or not.			
6. I read each sentence only once.			
7. I remember the ideas I want to remember.			
8. I read with one or more goals, reasons to direct my reading.			
9. Before I read, I look at the preface, contents, and index.			

When I Read	Always	Sometimes	Seldom
10. I pronounce each word to myself.			
11. I analyze the grammar in each sentence.			
12. I think about the main ideas I read.			
13. I look up the meaning of every word I don't know.			
14. I find reading an easy and enjoyable task.			

How does your Profile of Reading Habits look? Had you considered all the items listed as parts of reading?

After you finish the last exercise in this program, complete another Profile of Reading Habits and place an *O* in the column that describes your reading habits then. By comparing where you placed the *X* before taking the course and where you place the *O* after completing it, you can judge how much your efficiency has improved.

Course Preview

What Is Efficient Reading?

What do we mean when we talk about "reading efficiency"? Does it mean more than saving time by reading rapidly? What changes have to be made in the traditional reading process of translating visual symbols into words?

Reading effectively most certainly includes understanding the ideas the writer is trying to send. It includes organizing those ideas logically to remember them. But it also has to include processing the information as quickly as possible; we have so much to read and understand in what always seems too little time.

What About Rapid Eye Movement?

Reading is not a simple physical activity. You see nothing while your eyes are moving; to see, you must stop and

5

focus. Reading is much more than eye movement. When it is properly developed, the reading process is a thinking process. When you are reading to learn, you are constantly thinking, evaluating, judging, imagining, comparing, and reasoning. You are adding new information to previous knowledge, judging its value and validity, and comparing its use in solving problems or creating new horizons.

Training your eyes to move faster is useful in breaking restrictive reading habits—habits that slow you down and limit how much you remember. But eye movement alone will not increase your efficiency; the efficient reader is a thinking reader. Reading is a thinking process.

Why Are Reading Goals Important?

The effective reader has a purpose for reading, for taking time to go through the reading process. The more definite the purpose, the more effective the reading. Just as a purpose controls the way you drive an automobile—a leisurely drive through the country, a long trip in a short time, or a rush to a hospital emergency room—a purpose controls the way you read. Having a goal to reach means eliminating distractions that won't help you achieve that goal. As with driving, the methods you use vary with the goal you establish.

The ability to learn useful information quickly is the greatest single resource for reaching new goals in life. Your efficiency in handling the reading process can control your future. If you decide to improve your reading skills, you know that effort is required to change inefficiency to efficiency, to exchange habits that keep you from attaining your goal to those that support your purpose. Your goal is to increase both your rate of reading printed messages and your ability to understand and remember them.

How Much Comprehension?

When do you have enough comprehension? When you have achieved your goal. When you want to find a number in a phone directory, reading the entire book is, obviously, not an aid in achieving your goal quickly.

You may read for pleasure with no intention of using the information you read for any other purpose. Or you may read to find the sequence of events leading to a particular war. You may need to understand previous action taken before you can define a new policy, or you may want to know the metric equivalent for a pound. When you have found what you are seeking, you have satisfied your purpose for reading; you have as much comprehension as you need.

What Is Reading Versatility?

If to read is to understand, the reading method used to achieve the reader's purpose will be determined by the type of material and its difficulty. A book on biology will not be read at the same speed as a novel, even by a biologist. And the same biologist will use a different reading technique for a sports column; he'll read with versatility.

The versatile reader is also the efficient reader who reads in the best possible manner with the least waste of time. The versatile reader may be called the mature reader. He or she has conquered the problem of word-by-word reading, no longer feeling that each word should be studied.

Your goal is to develop into a versatile, efficient, mature reader—not just a rapid eye mover.

What Are the Obstacles to Overcome?

There are some roadblocks to developing reading efficiency: words, the way the words are used together, and the varied meanings we understand or interpret.

Words differ in length and in complexity. They are symbols that we must interpret according to our backgrounds; they have no meaning without interpretation. Look at any sentence in an unfamiliar language. Even when the same alphabet, the same form of letters, is used, the arrangement of those letters into words gives you no information unless you can understand the message being sent by the writer using the letter symbols; that is, unless the letters can be changed to words that give you thoughts. Words are useful only when they communicate ideas.

A complicated arrangement of words, sentences, or ideas will certainly affect the rate of reading. Compare ''John can read'' with ''John, our sixteen-year-old son, knows how to be a versatile reader, whether he reads fiction or nonfiction.'' The complexity of the second sentence will change the rate of recognition and the comprehension of the meaning.

There is also semantics. Semantics has to do with the different meanings of the same word. In the English language, the same word may have different meanings depending on its use in a sentence. Consider the word *run*. It may mean ''go quickly by moving the legs rapidly,'' or any of its 170 other meanings. They include the number of times a play is performed and a ravel in a knitted fabric such as hosiery.

Imagine how difficult this sentence is to understand for

someone not familiar with English: *The man was asked to take the stand and remain standing until he had taken the oath. He was a Quaker, and everyone knew what stand he would take*. If the reader referred to a dictionary, 62 meanings for *stand* could be found. Which would be the correct meaning?

To read efficiently, we must do more than recognize words rapidly.

Knowledge and Reading

Look out a window. You see an entire scene. The meaning you give it depends on your understanding of what you see—of the knowledge you have from your past experiences. Similarly, the style and difficulty of the material and the reader's experience and knowledge will influence the speed of comprehension.

Consider the meaning of the following nursery rhyme:

> Jack and Jill went up the hill
> To fetch a pail of water.
> Jack fell down and broke his crown,
> And Jill came tumbling after.

You probably thought it meant two children, sent to an illogical uphill location to obtain water, both fell down the hill. But how would your interpretation change if you knew that "Jack" was the common name applied to a corrupt king, and "Jill" was used to indicate his queen? Or what if "Jill" was *not* the queen but a woman of questionable reputation? Then "hill" might indicate power; "water" might mean "gains from corruption"; and whoever "Jill" is, she is dragged down with him—or causes the fall.

Yes, previous knowledge can influence the message you receive from reading, just as body language adds meaning to spoken messages; they provide you, the receiver, with more complete information to process, to think about.

Remembering

How do you remember new information? Memory courses offer numerous methods; so do programs for guided instruction and study techniques. Developing these skills helps us organize information and develop mental associations and visualizations for grouping facts, associating names, remembering numbers, and being able to tell a joke or deliver a speech.

All the techniques begin with setting a clear objective, a clearly defined purpose. A framework for the new information is built, and cues for recall are established. These include writing down cue words, working out associations with previous knowledge, grouping logical families of facts, and many others. The details vary, but memory relies on associations. So does effective reading.

The Process

Super Reading guides you in developing a success-ensured process for achieving your purpose for reading printed messages of all types. The articles used vary in type and content; you'll probably find some more interesting than others. But that range of subjects represents the variety of everyday reading tasks. We can't always limit our reading to what interests us. Keep in mind that we are developing a process, not attempting to entertain you.

The process has a definite sequence:

Survey the reading material to clarify what subject is discussed and the author's qualifications for presenting and organizing it for you. Although this is usually the first skill you use, it is not the first you'll learn. It's easier to apply after you have some background training.

Prepare to read:

Decide what questions you want answered using the six Question Words: *What, Who, When, Where, How,* and *Why.* These provide your **purposes** for reading.

Speculate on the answers to your questions to provide a framework for learning.

Select the reading skill you need to accomplish your purpose:

Skim-type reading to get brief, factual answers to questions asking *What, Who, When,* and *Where.*

Scan-type reading to see relationships, cause and effect, or other factual answers to *How* or *Why.*

Study-type reading when your *How* or *Why* questions require analysis and evaluation.

Rapid reading (pacing) to read fiction quickly, avoiding unnecessary details you don't need to remember.

Rapid reading nonfiction to apply your new skills to a **learning pattern** for processing nonfiction material.

Probably the two greatest changes in your reading habits will be the preparation for reading and the flexibility in the way you read different kinds of material. At first, preparation seems to add to the time needed to read. Don't be misled; when you master the skills, you'll be amazed at your improvement in speed, comprehension, and retention. You'll have acquired the ability to be in complete charge of what you read and how much you remember. You'll be an efficient, effective, skillful reader!

Study Plan

To complete this course successfully, it is important to use good study habits. You need a plan. To help you plan, let's look at the organization of the skill presentation.

Research has shown that reading-learning efficiently requires a series of skills. These skills are best learned in a building process, adding one skill at a time to those already developed until all skills are combined for efficient learning. For this reason, completing the program in the sequence it's presented is the most effective path to success. There are sound reasons for the order of skill presentation.

Each new section begins with very simple exercises to apply the new skill easily. The practice exercises gradually increase in difficulty to develop your ability to use the skill for a wide variety of reading materials.

Super Reading places great emphasis on practice. New skills require repeated application—playing golf or the piano *or* reading. The more you apply your new skills to *everything* you read, the greater will be your improvement. After you

13

complete the practice exercises in this book, practice with letters, reports, newspapers, magazines—all written material you encounter daily.

Remember these points when you are developing your study plan:

1. Set aside a certain time each day for learning and practicing.
2. When you read, concentrate on reading. Don't let your mind wander. If possible, work where there are no distractions.
3. Put each new skill to use as soon as possible. Consciously force yourself to use your new skills in reading books, magazines, newspapers, letters, or reports.
4. Use a dictionary to check meanings of words vital to understanding, but try to determine meanings from the context of the sentence first.
5. Read explanations and directions carefully. They provide a foundation for what follows.

The last skill presented in *Super Reading* is **rapid reading** or **pacing**. For skill development, you're asked to select some paperback books to practice reading fiction. You'll find it easier to concentrate on developing your skill rapidly if you choose books of 100 to 200 pages with simple plots and few characters. Complex plots may cause frustration when you're pushing yourself to read swiftly.

Enjoy *Super Reading*! Effective reading is the key to open whole worlds of knowledge, people, facts, dreams, theories, and fun.

The Nature of Questions

When you know *why* you are reading, you have a purpose for reading, a clearly defined reason for spending time and effort. Approaching any task with a plan increases the likelihood of directing the activity toward success.

Self-directed questions—planning ahead of time what you, the reader, want to get out of a selection—are the best means of directing your thinking. Knowing what answers you seek helps you find them quickly.

In their simplest form, questions seek the *What, Who, When, Where, How,* and *Why* of a situation. We call those six words "Question Words."

In the four questions below, reduce each question to one Question Word, even when the word is not in the question. Is the question asking *What? Who? When? Where? How?* or *Why?* Write the word in the right-hand column, then read the following paragraph to find the answer to write on the line after the question. Read just to find answers to the questions.

EXERCISE 1

1. Who is the "handsome one"?

   Answer: _____Paul_____

   Question Word: __Who__

2. What does he do in the group?

   Answer: _____

   Question Word: _____

3. In what way was he influenced by Elvis Presley?

   Answer: _____

   Question Word: _____

4. Why did he avoid girls?

   Answer: _____

   Question Word: _____

   The fans call Paul the handsome one, and he knows it. The others in the group call Paul "the Star." He does most of the singing and most of the wiggling, trying to swing his hips after the fashion of Elvis Presley, one of his boyhood idols. In the British equivalent of high school, Paul was mostly in the upper ranks scholastically, unlike the other Beatles. "He was like, you know, a goody-goody in school," remembers one of Paul's boyhood friends. He also, as another former classmate remembers him, was a "tubby little kid" who avoided girlish rejections by avoiding girls.

To check your answers, invert the Answer Key at the top of page 17.

Answer Key

Types of Questions

What is a question? The dictionary tells us it's a sentence in interrogative form addressed to someone in order to get information in reply. That definition certainly fits our need. When you use questions for defining your purpose for reading, you are asking the author to supply you with information. Your questions specify what information you seek, what specific facts you expect to learn.

Each of the six questions serves a particular need:

A **What** question asks for specific information. **Which** is sometimes substituted for **What**.
What happened?
What's the main idea?
Which is the best choice?
What is the best question to use first. It can ask for the subject of the story or article, the main idea or central theme. It's the most logical place to start your thinking.

A **Who** question asks for the identity of a person or a personified thing.
Who is involved?
Who can solve this problem?
Who caused it?

A **Who** question can be used as a starting point for your thinking if for some reason the answer to a **What** question isn't clear. In instructions, of course, the answer to **Who** is often you, the reader.

A **Where** question usually asks for the location, position, or place of a thing, event, or person.
Where is she writing?
Where is the trouble?
Where did it happen?

A **When** question usually asks for a time or a period of time or under what circumstances.
When will they arrive?
When can we change the procedure?
When did that unsettled condition exist?

A **How** question usually asks in what way or manner, by what means, to what extent or degree.
How do you address the president?
How did it happen?
In what condition is the car? (*How?*)
In what way does the machine operate the turntable? (*How?*)
How much damage was done?
By what means will you travel? (*How?*)

A **Why** question usually asks for what reason, for what cause.
Why did it happen?
Why is she leaving?
What reason does he have for changing the process? (*Why?*)
Why are we bankrupt?

To summarize, questions:

> Establish precise objectives for reading.
> Determine the level of comprehension necessary.
> Establish the direction for reading.
> Decide the reading skill to use.
> Indicate whether you want information or analysis.

Besides having their own individual categories of answers, questions divide reading methods by the types of answers they seek. By their nature, *What, Who, When*, and *Where* ask for literal information, information that is usually answered by a few words. Here is an example:

> The Civil War was costly, so the
> federal government in **Washington**   (*Where*)
> had to find a way to pay for it.
> Therefore, **Congress**   (*Who*)
> **adopted** the first of a series   (*What*)
> of revenue laws in
> **August 1861**. Among them—our   (*When*)
> **first income tax**.   (*What*)

It took 8 of the 40 words to quickly locate key information:

> Washington, Congress adopted, August 1861, first
> income tax.

Combining the answers to the questions in their briefest form, you can make a clear, concise summary of the statement:

> Congress adopted our first income tax in Washington
> in August 1861.

What you are doing is thinking in shorthand. You may want to call it speed thinking! If those are your only questions, your only reasons for reading, finding the answers as rapidly as possible is effective reading. If you also want to add *Why* after you have those first four answers, you can, of course, find that it was to pay for the Civil War. But you, the reader, decide what answers satisfy your need, and you don't waste time on the rest. That takes practice; we're used to reading everything.

Practice with the following brief stories. See if you can select the key *Question Words* as you did in the previous exercise. Write them in the spaces provided. Then find the answers to the questions as quickly as you can and write them on the *Answer* lines.

EXERCISE 2

1. Who is called Porpoise?   Question Word: _____
   Answer: _____

2. What does he do?   Question Word: _____
   Answer: _____

3. In what way will you learn
   how he started to swim?   Question Word: _____
   Answer: _____

4. At what point did he start
   using the lakes?   Question Word: _____
   Answer: _____

It's easy to see why George Grist is called Porpoise. It's just as easy to see why he's a swimmer instead of a baseball player. All you have to do is visit his hometown. There are fifteen small lakes in the countryside beyond the town limits. When George was still in grammar school, he learned to make use of them.

Answer Key

Question Words:
1. Who **2.** What **3.** How **4.** When

Answers:
1. George Grist **2.** Swims **3.** Visit his hometown
4. In grammar school

EXERCISE 3

1. Who made suggestions to the Admissions Board?   Question Word: _____
Answer: _____

2. In what way did the board react to the suggestions?   Question Word: _____
Answer: _____

3. When will the board put the suggestions into practice?   Question Word: _____
Answer: _____

According to Allen Smith, Representative Brown made a great many suggestions to the Admissions Board, some of which the board agreed to put into practice next year.

Answer Key

Answers:
1. Representative Brown
2. Agreed to put some into practice
3. Next year

Question Words:
1. Who **2.** How **3.** When

EXERCISE 4

1. Who ordered an end to the
   slowdown?   Question Word: _____
   Answer: _____

2. What reason did the judge
   have for issuing his order?   Question Word: _____
   Answer: _____

3. How long has service been
   interrupted?   Question Word: _____
   Answer: _____

4. Where has service been in-
   terrupted?   Question Word: _____
   Answer: _____

5. Who caused the slowdown?   Question Word: _____
   Answer: _____

6. In what way did the action
   of the repairmen influence
   the commuter line?   Question Word: _____
   Answer: _____

A federal judge has ordered an end to an alleged
slowdown by the Longwood Railroad car repairmen
that has disrupted service on the commuter line
for the last thirty days. He said the slowdown was
causing the public severe hardship.

Answer Key

EXERCISE 5

1. Who was the courageous
young man?   Question Word: _____
Answer: _____

2. In what way did he become
a skilled goldsmith?   Question Word: _____
Answer: _____

3. When did he make wooden
dolls?   Question Word: _____
Answer: _____

4. What did his father think of
his woodcarving?   Question Word: _____
Answer: _____

Grandfather was especially fond of talking about
Daniel Richard. "A wonderful, courageous young
man," he always began. "When he was just a
little boy, he made dolls and carts of wood. But
his father didn't want him wasting time on things
that would never earn him a living.

"By the time he was a little older than Pierre, he was quite a mechanic. They say he was actually a skilled goldsmith—no doubt because of his experience in woodcarving, which his father made the mistake of trying to discourage."

Answer Key

Didn't want him wasting his time
4. When he was just a little boy 3. woodcarving
in experience his of Because 2. Richard Daniel 1.
Answers:

What 4. When 3. How 2. Who 1.
Question Words:

Methods of Finding Answers

Not only do questions identify what you want to know; they also guide you to the most effective means of finding the answers.

Skim-type questions ask for literal, usually brief answers to the questions *What? Why? When? Where?* The questions don't require you to interpret or analyze, just to find the answer provided by the author. You now know that those four Question Words may not be in the question, but one is at least implied.

What can be asking the identity or purpose of something.
Who can be asking what or which person or people.
When can be asking at what time or under what circumstances.
Where can be asking the position or circumstance of a person or thing.

The questions give you clues to what you need to find quickly on a printed page:

> Repetition of the same word may indicate the subject being discussed.
> A name of a specific person or place will be capitalized.
> Numerals are easy to see on a page of words.
> Words in the answer may match those in the question.

Using these cues increases your speed in finding the answers—and, consequently, your reading rate.

Scan-type questions ask *How?* or *Why?* You are still looking for what the author gives as answers, but usually more than one or two words are needed. You may be looking for reasons, causes, steps in a process, or summaries of facts. In **scan-type** questions you still rely on the writer's facts, with no evaluation on your part.

> *How* may be asking in what manner, in what condition, to what degree (how much?), or in which order.
> *Why* may imply words like "explain the effects," "list causes," or "give the reasons."

Your reading rate is slower for **scan-type** reading than for **skim-type**, of course, because you're looking for more facts.

Study-type questions also ask *How?* and *Why?*, but for these questions you are asked to analyze and evaluate and consider your past knowledge and experience. This is critical reading, the slowest and most demanding.

> *How* may really be asking that you "analyze the reasons," "evaluate the reaction or the process," or "interpret the decision."

Why may imply "give your reasons for agreeing or disagreeing," "evaluate the results," or "estimate future results."

EXERCISE 6

You have learned the six Question Words. Now you'll identify the types of reading needed to find the answers to the questions. In the column titled *Question Words,* write what question is being asked.

In the column at the right, identify what type of reading each question requires: **skim, scan,** or **study.**

	Question Word	Type of Reading
Example: What are the five largest cities in Japan?	What	Skim
1. Where did Pat get her dog?	_____	_____
2. What position does Joe play?	_____	_____
3. Who invented the elevator?	_____	_____
4. Where did the train jump the track?	_____	_____
5. Why didn't Fred graduate?	_____	_____
6. In how many ways is the car unsafe?	_____	_____

7. Why are doctors against smoking?   _____ _____

8. How did the senator gain national acclaim?   _____ _____

Questions 1, 2, 3, and 4 are **skim-type** questions. They ask for brief answers in the words of the author.

Questions 5, 6, 7, and 8 are **scan-type** questions using *How* or *Why*.

Study-type questions also ask *How* or *Why*. Let's see if you can tell the difference between the **scan** *How* and *Why* and **study** *How* and *Why* questions. Remember that **scan-type** questions ask only what the writer provides, and **study-type** questions ask for some evaluation from you. For some, you must turn instructions (describe, illustrate) into questions to determine the type of reading needed.

9. Why is the inventory short?   _____ _____

10. Why should we incorporate an accounting department in both buildings?   _____ _____

11. Why are quick responses necessary in hockey?   _____ _____

12. Why did England enter into the alliance?   _____ _____

13. In what way did the senator significantly contribute to the debate?   _____ _____

14. How do you think the United States improved its mail service? _____ _____

15. Do you think the trend toward wide lapels in men's suits will continue? Why or why not? _____ _____

16. Describe the main philosophical differences between Red China and Nationalist China. _____ _____

17. How can a student read faster? _____ _____

18. Illustrate the difference between the foreign-made compacts and the American-made. _____ _____

19. Describe the sales procedure used and the steps necessary to complete it. _____ _____

20. What is the difference between pro sports and college sports? _____ _____

The **scan-type** questions are 9, 11, 12, 17, and 20. The **study-type** are 10, 13, 14, 15, 16, 18, and 19. Can you see the difference? There are clues that help you.

Study-type questions have words that require more explanation, definition, or even your reaction and judgment. For example, questions 18 and 19 ask you to "illustrate" and "describe." Question 13 asks you to judge the significance. These demand more time and thought than just picking up answers from your reading.

Scan-type questions are usually shorter in length and more direct in what they ask you to supply. In question 11 you are asked why quick reactions are necessary in hockey. This would require a short answer taken directly from the reading. Although the reasons might not be listed in consecutive sentences, you wouldn't have to analyze or evaluate what the writer gave you.

Remember:

What, Who, When, Where..........tell us to **skim** read.
How and Why ....tell us to **scan** read.
How and Why plus the implied "explain, describe, evaluate, interpret" ....tell us to **study** read.

Reading Quickly and Efficiently

Keeping in mind that your reason for reading will determine in great measure how fast you will read, practice with the following stories. Before each exercise you will find a question. Read as rapidly as you can to find the answer, *keeping the question firmly in mind for your focus*. After you write the answer—as briefly as possible, not in sentence form—list any other information you can remember. Do **not** go back to look for facts.

You'll be surprised by how rapidly you can read when you really try. You'll be just as surprised at how much information you can recall.

Suggested answers to all exercises are on page 265.

EXERCISE 7

Question: *What* is the main idea of the following article?

Answer: _____

Facts you remember: _____

_____

_____

"Stock-car drivers make better drivers on the road. They're more safety conscious because they must build safety right into their cars. In fact, the cars are subject to state inspection."

Stock-car driving has contributed to modern auto safety. Several devices brought into widespread use after being utilized by car racing include rear-view mirrors, seat belts, and shoulder straps.

Engines have improved, too, but some auto designers failed to take safety into account when substituting more powerful engines. Of the new sports cars, Ruberti quips, "You can't put a 427 on roller skates."

Despite the accent on safety, car racing offers thrills for the entire family, according to Ruberti.

"It's difficult to pick the winner; races are won on the turns. Even when somebody's way out ahead there's always good racing on the track, even if they're trying for fourteenth or fifteenth place.

"Safety lies in good driving; and safety precautions don't necessarily lie in speed. Speeds are great; running into a wall can mean a good smash-up. But sometimes running too cautiously is worse than driving too deep,'' he explained. ''Stock-car drivers aren't naturally rough, though they're more competitive.

''I like the competition of stock-car racing. There's self-satisfaction in winning a feature. It feels pretty good,'' he ended up simply. ''A majority of the racers don't make expenses. They do it for sport and love of it.''

Reprinted from the *Vineland Times Journal*, Vineland, New Jersey.

EXERCISE 8

Allow one minute to read the following. Then answer your question and list the facts you remember.

Question: *Where* does the novel take place?

Answer: _____

Facts you remember: _____
_____
_____

Keepers of the Obelisk

The diplomat Metternich kept telling the Congress of Vienna back in 1815 that Italy is only a geographical expression. That was a long time ago, of course, and things didn't work out quite as Metternich foresaw. But today Italy seems to have developed into something almost as surprising: an abstraction created by skylarking novelists. In this sportive land zany villagers, unpredictable politicians, and assorted oddballs of both sexes and all ages abound, and hardly anything seems too preposterous for belief.

Consider Howard Shaw's novel *Keepers of the Obelisk*. A former United States Foreign Service officer in Italy, Mr. Shaw is an old hand at guided tours of this region. A few years ago he wrote a highly successful comic novel called *The Crime of Giovanni*, adapted into a considerably less successful Broadway musical called *Bravo Giovanni*.

Keepers of the Obelisk is set in a dusty town in the Sabine hills near Rome. It is the lot of this village, which bears the grandiose name of Regina Coeli, to be the site of an accidental but amazing discovery—an Egyptian obelisk buried amid the water mains of its central piazza. As a consequence, not only is the town water supply shut off (to the considerable advantage of the local wineshop), but Regina Coeli is inundated by waves of curious and dubious personages, including the Honorable Zingabelli, a profit-seeking politico from Rome; Prof. Nicola Pamfredoni, a savant with a secret distaste for all things Egyptian; and an army of Arab and Afro-Asian dignitaries overwhelmed by the newly found relic of their glorious heritage.

It's a promising situation, but Mr. Shaw's townsfolk are generally a colorless bunch, and the hilarity of their efforts to get rid of the obelisk and regain their tranquility soon becomes contrived and artificial. Even the Engineer Robotti, the most harebrained and engaging of the villagers, gets hopelessly swallowed up in the plot spaghetti when he encounters, for no good reason, a decaying French princess who suddenly turns up.

Reprinted from *The National Observer,* with permission from Dow Jones and Co., Inc.

EXERCISE 9

Question: *When* does choking occur?

Answer: _____

Facts you remember: _____

_____

_____

How to Save a Choking Victim

Stand behind the victim and wrap your arms around his waist. Allow the upper body to hang forward.

Grab your fist with your other hand and place the thumb side of your fist against the victim's abdomen, slightly above the navel and below the rib cage.

Press your fist forcefully into the victim's abdomen with a quick upward thrust. Repeat several times if necessary.

If the victim is lying on his back, face him and kneel astride his thighs. With one hand on top of the other, place the heel of your bottom hand on the abdomen slightly above the navel and below the rib cage. Press forcefully into the abdomen with a quick upward thrust.

Each year an estimated 4,000 people in the United States alone die from food strangulation.

Choking occurs when food is sucked into the windpipe instead of being swallowed. Laughter while eating, excessive alcohol consumption, and children playing with candy or small objects in their mouths are the most common causes of choking.

This simple and effective maneuver, approved by the American Medical Association, forces the diaphragm upward, compressing air into the lungs and forcing the object from the windpipe.

Points to Remember:

• Before performing this maneuver it is important to determine whether the victim is suffering from a heart attack or food strangulation. The heart attack victim can both speak and breathe. A choking victim can do neither.

• The maneuver should be used on children with a lessening in the amount of pressure used.

• If no help is at hand a choking victim can perform this maneuver on himself by pressing his own fist upward as described.

• Act promptly in using these measures. A person choking on food will die in only four minutes unless *you* act to save him.

EXERCISE 10

Question: *Who* united Norway into one nation?

Answer: _____

Facts you remember: _____
_____
_____

Norway, situated in the northernmost part of Western Europe, is a modern, industrialized, democratic state with a population of 4 million.

Norway has in the twentieth century been developed by its people into a country with one of the world's highest standards of living. The mainstay of its economy is an expanding industry based on advanced technology.

Norway was united into one nation at the end of the ninth century by the Viking king Harald the Fair-Hair. During the following centuries Norwegian Vikings, in their long-ships of revolutionary design, established settlements throughout the North Sea's bordering lands and made commercial and military forays to even more distant countries.

Leiv Eiriksson, a Viking chieftain who had settled in Iceland, set sail further westward across the Atlantic Ocean in the year 1000 and became the first European to step ashore in North America. Present-day archeological excavations indicate that Viking settlements existed along the coast of Newfoundland. In the United States, Leiv Eiriksson Day is celebrated by Presidential Proclamation on October 9th of each year.

Reprinted from *What You Should Know about Norway*, published by the Norwegian Information Service in the United States.

EXERCISE 11

Question: *Why* was he sent?

Answer: _____

Facts you remember: _____

_____

_____

When Commodore Matthew C. Perry sailed his black-hulled fleet on its famous mission to Japan in 1853, he carried with him elaborate instructions from the Secretary of the Navy that specifically cited the wreck of the *Lawrence* and the "great barbarity" her crew suffered. Perry was sent to conclude a treaty with Japan that would insure, in President Millard Fillmore's phrase, "friendship, amity, and intercourse" between the two nations—meaning coaling stations for U.S. ships and trade agreement for U.S. merchants. But the first stated aim of the proposed treaty was to provide humane treatment for shipwrecked Americans. And should persuasion fail, the State Department told Perry, he was to inform the Japanese "that if any acts of cruelty should hereafter be practiced upon the citizens of this country, whether by the government or by the inhabitants of Japan, they will be severely chastised." Perry found that the intimation of force was enough; forts painted on silk curtains were no match for Yankee armaments. The treaty he concluded in 1854 assured decent treatment for shipwrecked sailors; the ports of Shimoda and Hakodate were designated for provisioning American ships; and, within a few years, Japan was at last opened for commercial exploration.

Reprinted from "Castaways on Forbidden Shores," by Robert Gallagher, which appeared in *American Heritage,* June 1968. The American Heritage Publishing Co., Inc., New York, NY.

•

Using the Six Question Words Together

Up to this point we have been using only one of the Question Words in each exercise. Now we are going to use *all* Question Words for each article. By using all six words, we employ a more complete approach for extracting the important facts and doing it more efficiently. *What* (is the subject) is usually the most helpful question to ask first.

Remember: Beginning now, every time you read, ask yourself, "Why am I reading this?" that translates into, "What do I need or want to know from this reading?" The six questions help you define your exact purpose and direct your reading. The results are better understanding and longer retention.

Notice how the 17 italicized words in the following article help you gather the main facts.

What?	Immigration program	Where?	Australia
Who?	Australian government	Why?	Need for accelerated population growth

When? <u>1969–70</u>   How? <u>Traveled with Federal Government help</u>

Where Immigration had always been a feature of *Australia's* development. At the end of World War II there was an urgent need *for accelerated population growth*, both to enable more rapid development of the nation's resources and to offset the demographic trough caused by the low birthrate of the 1930's.   **Why**

There was also the urgent call to provide refuge for many thousands of Europeans made homeless by the war, and large numbers of families in Britain and Europe were seeking more satisfying lives and opportunities in new homelands.

From these circumstances emerged the decision by the *Australian government* to embark on a large-scale *immigration program* which could be coordinated with other aspects of national development.   **Who** **What**

Since then, all major political and social groups have supported this policy as an important means of achieving Australia's economic and social objectives.

The immigration program for *1969–70* provided for 175,000 settlers, but it was expected to be exceeded. It was intended that 119,000 of these *would travel with Federal Government help* toward their passage costs.   **When**   **How**

There are 171 words in this article, but only 17 or about 10 percent are needed to zero in on the answers to the key questions, the vital facts. Unless we have a need for more details, we can eliminate the other 90 percent of the words. We have accomplished our purpose efficiently.

EXERCISE 12

Use all six Question Words as your purpose for reading the following article. Underline the words you use as answers.

In seeking your answers, take two or three questions and read just until you find the answers. Then repeat for two or three more questions. You will find, of course, that not all articles have answers to all six questions.

What is the subject of the article? _____
Who is the person or people involved? _____
When is it flown? _____
Where was it flown? _____
How is it formed? _____
Why were these symbols chosen? _____

The New Zealand Ensign

The flag of New Zealand, officially known as the New Zealand Ensign, was adopted in 1901. The New Zealand Ensign has the Union Jack of Great Britain in the top left-hand corner and the Southern Cross on a blue background. It is the recognised flag for use on shore and on government vessels.

The Southern Cross is a famous constellation visible in the Southern Hemisphere and, for a distance, North of the Equator. It is possible to find out the hour of the night by the position of the Southern Cross in the sky. The two stars forming the vertical limb give an approximate position of the South Pole.

Occasions on which the New Zealand Ensign is flown include New Zealand Day on 6 February and Anzac Day, 25 April. Flags are flown to mark the birthday of Queen Elizabeth II; on her actual birthday, 21 April, and on the day of official observance in New Zealand, the first Monday in June. Flags are also flown in Wellington for the opening of Parliament. New Zealand no longer has a federal system, but on the Anniversary Day of each Province, flags are still flown throughout the Province concerned.

Printed for the New Zealand Embassy, Washington, DC.

How many words did you underline? _____
There are about 200 words in the article. Roughly, what percent of the words did you use to answer the questions? _____
Do you see the value of the questions for obtaining information quickly and efficiently? _____

EXERCISE 13

Underline and count the number of words you use to answer
the six questions in this article.

What? _____   Where? _____
Who? _____   How? _____
When? _____   Why? _____

In a letter to the Editor of the *Journal of the
American Medical Association,* Dr. Frank Perlman
of the University of Oregon Medical School points
out that many of the tests of sensitivity to penicillin may not be as perfect as they had been thought
to be. He reports experiences with four patients
who had not reacted to the skin test with penicilloyl-
polylysine or with the penicillanic acid ordinarily
used. Each patient reacted when scratch tested
with ordinary penicillin G.

In one patient there was a general reaction by
which is usually meant hives and asthma as well
as other signs of allergy affecting all of the body.
In another patient there was anaphalactic shock.
Only "heroic measures" saved the life of the
patient. Had these or the other two patients received penicillin on the basis of the negative tests
routinely done, they might have died.

Dr. Perlman states that history of penicillin
sensitivity is enough evidence for the non-use of
the drug. Should there be a history of penicillin
allergy and there is no other drug which can
replace the penicillin, then the tests should be

done by those who are experienced in the performance of all of the types of tests for allergy to penicillin.

Reprinted from *The Asthmastic Patient*, published by The Asthma Research Foundation, Inc., Boston, MA.

How many words did you underline? _____
There are 214 words in the article.

Now you have an idea of the importance of having a purpose for reading. When you use questions to establish a purpose, you learn much more in less time.

Important: Take any nonfiction material, preferably something you need to remember. Use the questions to set your purpose, and notice how much more efficient you are in learning information.

Speculating

It's time to pause to review what you have just learned and to introduce a new step in the reading-learning process.

First you studied **The Nature of Questions**, using questions to establish your purpose for reading. You practiced reading for a single purpose (answering one question) and moved on to a broader purpose using all six questions—giving you new skills in reading quickly and efficiently.

Let's imagine what goes on in your mind now as you start to read. Step 1 is to **set purpose**. When you have this step firmly in mind, you are ready to learn step 2 in the reading/thinking process: to **speculate** or to predict.

What do we mean when we say "speculate"? Before you start to read, you predict, speculate, or guess what the author is going to tell you. One of the real pleasures we get from reading mystery stories is predicting who did it and how the villain will be caught.

Predicting is just as important, however, in reading a newspaper, magazine, or required reading in textbooks and journals. When you predict, you alert your mind to a challenge. You look at the title or chapter heading or any other clues such as pictures or graphs, and you predict or guess what the material will tell you. Then you are involved. The thought game has started. The odds that you will be right and win the mental challenge are usually against you, and that's good. It's good because when you lose this mental game and are wrong, your ability to *understand* and *remember* what the author said will be greatly increased.

It sounds like we are saying, "It's all right to be wrong," and that's exactly what we *are* saying in connection with **speculating**. We learn and remember more from our mistakes than from the things we get right. Think about it for a minute from your own experience. You remember your bad golf shots better than your good ones. When you were in school and left the class after taking a test, you remembered the questions you missed rather than the ones you answered correctly.

Think about **speculating** from another standpoint. When you **speculate**, you establish a reference point from which to measure what the author is telling you. You become a critical thinker, constantly evaluating the author's message against your own information and experience. You can see the importance of a mental reference point by taking a ruler and trying to measure an inch without having a starting point. You can read without **speculating**, but your *comprehension* and *retention* will be greatly improved if you have a reference point.

Perhaps you hadn't thought about it, but most of us have been trained *not* to predict or speculate. In school we didn't raise our hands to volunteer an answer unless we were pretty sure we were correct. We didn't want to be embarrassed by being wrong.

Yet, it may surprise you to learn that there are huge buildings all over the world built on the premise that we learn and make progress only when we **speculate** and are free to be wrong. Surely you've seen many of the buildings; they usually have big signs saying RESEARCH CENTER. The work done in them has one purpose: to prove that predictions (called "hypotheses") are either right or wrong.

We hope you understand the value of **speculating** and become comfortable with the possibility of being wrong when you **speculate**. Remember the turtle: he only makes progress when he sticks out his neck.

You are now ready to develop three new skills to help you to accomplish your purpose efficiently. Each of these skills has a role in your versatile reading: to decide whether to use **skim-, scan-,** or **study-type** reading. When you have mastered all three, you'll be a flexible, mature reader who can match the appropriate skill to your purpose for reading.

You'll practice **speculating** while you are learning **skim-type** reading.

Skim-Type Reading

First Level of Comprehension— Literal Meanings

Most people use the term "skim reading" without really knowing that it is a specific reading skill. Their use of the term is frequently an excuse for not gaining adequate comprehension or retention from what they read.

Let's correctly define the term **skim-type** reading:

> **Skim-type** reading is reading swiftly and lightly, looking for literal or factual information. **Skim-type** reading is used when our purpose is to search for a few words that answer the questions *What? Who? Where? When?*

Understanding what **skim-type** reading is, you can see how inefficient it is to read an entire article or book word by word. Besides being slow, that method provides no organization of the thoughts that meet your personal reason for reading, that answer the questions you need to have answered. **Speculating** builds the framework for evaluating that information.

To practice the entire process, proceed through the following **skim-type** exercises as follows:

1. Make sure you have your *purpose* clearly in mind. In these exercises, your purpose is set for you in the questions before each article.

2. **Speculate** on the answers to the questions. We've supplied some samples for the first exercises.

3. **Skim** read the article, moving your eyes rapidly down the column of print until you spot a word or two that answers your *purpose* questions.

Because you are developing your **skim-type** reading skills, these exercises aren't timed. Later you'll work to develop a higher rate of speed. But do push yourself to complete the **purpose setting–speculating–answering** process rapidly.

EXERCISE 14

Our Question: **1.** Who is the Poet of the Musconetcong?
Our Speculation: Robert Frost
Your Speculation: _____

Our Question: **2.** Where is the Musconetcong?
Our Speculation: In New Mexico
Your Speculation: _____

Poet of the Musconetcong

Did you know that Walt Whitman, Bret Harte and Joyce Kilmer were New Jersey poets? If you didn't, don't fret. Most New Jerseyans aren't aware that this small corner of America has a long tradition of providing a home and inspiration for bards great and near great.

New Jersey can point to Revolutionary period poet-patriots like Francis Hopkinson of Bordentown and Philip Freneau of Monmouth County, who took up the sword along with the pen. A few generations later, Bret Harte won renown while living in Morristown, and Walt Whitman penned some of his greatest work in Camden.

The name of New Brunswick's Joyce Kilmer, author of "Trees," is familiar to generations of American schoolchildren.

Joyce probably would have gone on to capture New Jersey's natural beauty in verse were his destiny not decided in his death on a battlefield in France in 1918. But the state was not to be denied a bard to sing the praises of its woods and streams and its common folk.

The singer was A. M. Sullivan, New Jersey's twentieth century "poet emeritus," a little-known writer, but one whose achievements mark him as likely successor to Whitman, Harte, and Kilmer.

Born in Harrison just after the turn of the century, Sullivan was raised in the rural Warren County village of Oxford, where his father ran a country store. Sullivan himself eventually settled in Montclair. But, it was the half-century of summers spent at a family home on the banks of the Musconetcong River near Hackettstown that provided the inspiration for much of his New Jersey verse.

His 1968 collection *Songs of the Musconetcong and Other Poems of New Jersey* forms a poetic scrapbook. The author takes a scenic sojourn through the four seasons on his beloved river and surrounding hills. Along the route his poems explore the landscape, from blackberry to the earthworm. From time to time, he takes a poetic snapshot of local culture in works like "The County Fair."

In "Midnight Caravan" he leaves the rural setting and heads east in a poem about the highway, U.S. 1. Sullivan describes trucks lumbering along the road from Philadelphia to their destination in New York City, along the way passing old villages that "ache with the thunder of wheels, the beating of tappet and piston."

In addition to his poetry on New Jersey, Sullivan wrote on philosophy, history, science and industry. In all he produced some ten collections of poetry, earning applause from critics and contemporaries the likes of Edgar Lee Masters.

In 1976, four years before his death, Sullivan was awarded the Poetry Society of America's highest honor, a gold medal of achievement. With this honor the "Bard of the Musconetcong" joined the ranks of such nationally loved literary greats as Robert Frost and Edna St. Vincent Millay.

Reprinted from *Tel-News*, New Jersey Bell

Answers: 1. _____
        2. _____

EXERCISE 15

Our Question: **1.** Who are Icarus and Arthur Clarke?
Our Speculation: Ancient and modern writers
Your Speculation: _____

Our Question: **2.** For what are they noted?
Your Speculation: _____

From Icarus to Arthur Clarke

*Space haunted man's oldest dreams and early
civilizations created stories about it. Now called science
fiction, it's often more science than fiction.*

Man has gazed at the stars ever since he could
stand erect; and man was dreaming about traveling
among the stars long before he dared to dream of
crossing oceans. Earth-bound though he was, his
mind could soar, and it soared into the heavens.
There he saw the gods, Jupiter and Juno and
Mars, and, in another age, another religion, Jehovah.

Man is a dreamer, and, even in this age of cost
accounting when there are those who insist on
putting a price tag on every dream, asking, "Yes,
but does it have any practical value?" man insists
on letting his mind soar. He devours science
fiction.

Though the possibility of realizing the dreams
is new, science fiction is not an invention of the
20th century. Man was weaving his dreams into
stories as far back as even legend recalls. The
ancient Greeks in their mythology told each other
the story of Icarus. Daedalus, father of Icarus,
fashioned a pair of wings for his son from birds'
feathers held together by wax. Daedalus warned
him not to fly too high and especially not to fly
too near the sun, but curiosity overcame him. The
sun melted the wax, and Icarus plunged to his
death.

Today science-fiction writers tell of visits from
other planets by demons with the power to destroy
the minds and souls of men. It's an idea that is
found as far back as Plutarch. He believed that

demons inhabiting the moon occasionally journeyed to earth to wreak havoc. He suggested that Socrates was such a demon.

The sophist Lucian of Samosata, who lived in 2nd-century Greece, wrote the first two stories of space travel. In the first, the hero was sailing beyond the Pillars of Hercules when he was swept up by a whirlwind. His boat was carried to the moon atop a whirling waterspout. In the second, the hero learned to fly with one wing from an eagle and one from a vulture. Taking off from Mount Olympus, he reached the moon. From there he flew to heaven, a three-day trip, only to find that he was unwelcome. The gods resented his presence, and Mercury returned him to earth.

The ancients, of course, had only a limited knowledge of science, so the science fiction of ancient times had only a fleeting relation to reality. With the invention of the telescope at the debut of the 17th century, however, this began to change. Man continued to dream, but increasingly his dreams became founded on fact. They became prophecies, many of which have since come true.

Many of the great science-fiction writers of modern times have been well grounded in science, some have actually been scientists. In fact, the first great science-fiction writer of modern times was Johannes Kepler, the astronomer. He wrote *Somnium*, a story of a voyage to the moon that anticipated many of the problems confronted by space scientists who came after him.

Even in 1634, 269 years before the Wright brothers and 323 years before Sputnik, Kepler realized that flying within the earth's atmosphere

and traveling in outer space could not be alike,
and he anticipated many of the special problems
that the space voyager would face—the cold and
the lack of air. Writing 31 years before Sir Isaac
Newton developed his theory of gravity, Kepler
recognized that both the earth and the moon
exerted what he called "a magnificent influence."
In *Somnium*, Kepler's hero reaches a point in
space where the magnetic influence of the moon
exceeds that of the earth and pulls him to a
landing.

As a scientist who also wrote science fiction,
Johannes Kepler was the forerunner of men like
Dr. Arthur C. Clarke, today's flourishing popularizer
of space. Cyrano de Bergerac was an amateur
scientist. The swashbuckling poet, playwright,
philosopher and swordsman, like Kepler, anticipated
Newton in the possibilities of gravitation. Besides
predicting the development of the parachute and
the tape recorder and speculating on how life
could be sustained in solar temperatures, he also
hit on the principle of reaction rockets when he
conceived of a novel way of getting into space—a
box powered by a cluster of rockets.

Reprinted by permission of *Forbes* magazine. Photos
by Bettman Archives.

Answers: **1.** _____
_____

2. _____
_____

EXERCISE 16

Sometimes our reading is in chart form. Before we can study the chart intelligently, we must identify the material with skim-type questions.

Our Question: **1.** What method has the best total rating?
Your Speculation: _____

Our Question: **2.** What type of information is provided going across? Down?
Your Speculation: _____

Rank Order of Effectiveness of Methods in Achieving Six Training Goals

9 low _____ 1 high

Answers: **1.** _____
_____

        2. _____
_____

Rank Order of Effectiveness of Method in Achieving 6 Training Goals

9 low ⟶ 1 high

Goals Method	Knowledge Acquisition		Changing Attitudes		Problem-Solving		Inter-Personal Skills		Participant Acceptance		Knowledge Retention		TOTALS		TOTAL
	L	R	L	R	L	R	L	R	L	R	L	R	L	R	
Case Study	2	4	4	5	1	1	4	5	2	1	2	4	15	20	35
Conference	3	1	3	3	4	5	3	4	1	5	5	2	19	20	39
Lecture	9	8	8	7	9	7	8	8	8	8	8	3	50	41	91
Business Games	6	5	5	4	2	2	5	3	3	2	6	7	27	23	50
Films	4	6	6	6	7	9	6	6	5	4	7	5	35	36	71
Prog. Instr.	1	3	7	8	6	6	7	7	7	9	1	1	29	34	63
Role Play	7	2	2	2	3	3	2	1	4	3	4	5	22	16	38
Sensitivity	8	7	1	1	5	4	1	2	6	6	3	9	24	29	53
TV Lecture	5	9	9	9	8	8	9	9	9	7	9	8	49	50	99

(L) left side of each column:

Carroll, Stephen, et al., "The Relative Effect of Training Methods—Expert Opinion and Research." Personnel Psychology, Vol. 25, 1972, pp. 495-509.

(R) right side of each column:

Newstrom, John, "Evaluating the Effectiveness of Training Methods", Personnel Administrator, January, 1980, pp. 55-60.

EXERCISE 17

Our Question: **1.** What makes giving penicillin undesirable?
Your Speculation: _____.

Our Question: **2.** If penicillin is not given when a patient has a strep throat, how much longer will the patient remain ill?
Your Speculation: _____

Our Question: **3.** What makes a throat culture an inaccurate indication of a strep throat?
Your Speculation: _____

Sore Throat Problem

How should a physician diagnose and treat a severe sore throat? Here is some information. Assuming that unusual cases are ruled out, the sore throat may be caused either by bacteria (usually streptococci, in which case the condition is commonly called strep throat) or by a virus. If the sore throat is in fact caused by streptococci, the treatment is penicillin, rest, and symptomatic relief (gargling, for example). If it is caused by a virus, rest and symptomatic relief are all that a physician should prescribe. Failure to treat a strep throat may result in a serious disease, such as glomerulonephritis or rheumatic heart disease. Treatment with penicillin (whether correct or incorrect) may result in a penicillin reaction, which usually consists of two to seven days of extreme discomfort from a rash and itching. In very rare cases, penicillin reaction takes the form of a fulminating illness leading to death. Therefore, it is not desirable to give penicillin needlessly.

If the patient has a strep throat and penicillin treatment is delayed by a day, the patient may remain ill for one extra day. If penicillin is never given, he may remain ill for about two extra days. In any case, the patient will be ill for at least five days.

In addition, both viral and strep sore throats are contagious. However, in the case of strep, the probability of contagion is decreased by penicillin treatment.

The physician may take a throat culture which will indicate the presence or absence of streptococci—the results of the culture are usually known one day later. This culture may not give perfect information because the bacteria may die before they are "planted" and because the presence of streptococci in the throat does not necessarily indicate that the sore throat is caused by the bacteria.

Thus, the physician's immediate problem is to decide whether to take a culture and whether to prescribe penicillin on the first day.

Reprinted from *Analysis for Decision Making,* by Howard Raiffa, Ph.D., Harvard Business School. Published by Learn Incorporated, Mount Laurel, NJ.

Answers: **1.** _____
         2. _____
         3. _____

EXERCISE 18

Our Question: **1.** Who is Thomas Rice?
Your Speculation: _____

Our Question: **2.** What was the biggest thing in U.S. theater from 1850 to 1880?
Your Speculation: _____

Our Question: **3.** What kind of bootlegging involved Bert Williams?
Your Speculation: _____

A Lot of Laughs, A Lot of Changes
by Godfrey Cambridge

"...the line that leads to Moms Mabley, Nipsey Russell, Dick Gregory, Bill Cosby and myself can be traced back to the social satire of slave humor, back even through minstrelsy. ....I am not about to deny this history because it happens to be filled with ninny-grinning black comedians."

There I am, stage center, and everybody's on the edge of their seats, expectant. And somebody in the audience whispers, "Spht, spht . . . that's Godfrey Cambridge." Only thing, nobody knows my predicament, standing in the middle of the set, perspiring like crazy. The thing is, I can't remember my lines. All I think of is the voice over my shoulder . . . someone saying . . . "What you're really doing, Godfrey, is playing the most important part in the play. You're the best friend of Rock Hudson, see? Better than Doris Day even, and what you do is . . . while you talk with him about his problems, you make the bed, press his pants, take his clothes to the laundry, because without you picking up his socks, supporting him in this role, he would be nothing, got it?''

So there I am, center stage, and there is no more voice, but I got it. I pick up on the line this time, the whole dreary historical characterization. It's like I come in, shuffle to the footlights, roll my eyes, doff my head and say, ''Yassuh, boss, telephone is ringing,'' or ''Mr. So and So, the telephone is for you, suh.''

Now that was a nightmare, and I can do without that kind of headache except to poke fun at the idiot who wrote the scripts. Only this bad dream, this derisive stereotype existed as the only job opportunity for Negro comics as late as a few years ago. These days no one would dare propose this artificial image, leastways I hope not. Still, hard as it is to swallow, this was the narrow box within which the Negro comedian of the past had to contain his talent or else not work at all. Some of us, luckily enough, have come a long way from this.

Usually in interviews I get the question, ''How come this current rash of black comics making it in the big time all of a sudden?'' And from this question I realize what little really is known about the tradition of the black comedian. Like man, we've been working right along, taking what we could get. I think it was Sammy Davis who once said, ''If it hadn't been for Hattie McDaniel, there would possibly be no Diana Sands; if there were no Stepin Fetchit or Mantan Moreland, there would be no Sidney Poitier," and I think that has been pretty much the case for the black performer.

The line that leads to Moms Mabley, Nipsey Russell, Dick Gregory, Bill Cosby and myself can be traced back to the social satire of slave humor, back even through minstrelsy, through countless attempts to cast off completely the artificial stereotype of that fantasy. Consequently, I am not about to deny this history because it happens to be filled with ninny-grinning Negro comedians. I know the expedient mockery of tambourines and banjos hidden in that grin, and the price those comedians paid whenever they tried to expand the scope of Negro comedy despite prevailing restrictions. My connection, the link between those of us today and our past, is the continuation of a proud, developing tradition, one evolving toward an honest and accurate expression of our experience as blacks in this kaleidoscope of America. Since we black comics seem to be getting closer to our own truth, I have for a long time wanted to survey these points, so we can learn how much further to dig in our attempts to bury it.

To begin, we might as well jump into the grease bucket, some of us coming up darker than we are, because everyone, all comedians, wore burnt cork in those early days.

The whole thing started with Jim Crow, which at the time just before the Civil War was less a description of segregation and more the title of a musical farce popularized by a white comedian. Thomas Rice was his name, and it was his original Jim Crow musical that set the pattern for the minstrel. Tom Rice's "Negro" was the figment of a bad comedy writer's imagination. Nobody likes to have himself written about by somebody who knows the least about him. And this is exactly what this starving actor did to make money, which incidentally is why I am also against actors starving.

Anyway, I know the digs and slurs of the minstrel show only too well. You know, the so-called coons and the cat in the tail coat who comes out says, "Gentlemen be seated," and Mr. Bones saying, "Why is a journey round de world like a cat's tail" Answer: "Cuz it's fur to de end of it." Now come on, baby, I mean really!!! That's not funny at all, just corny. But this was the kind of exaggerated nonsense minstrel shows interpreted to the outside world as Negro humor.

Simply stated, producers were interpreting the Negro theatrically, always for the entertainment of white people who played us in blackface in a way that made them happy. You see, they had to create a character their own society could accept and feel safe about, when actually there was a lot of anxiety with slave insurrectionists like Nat Turner and Denmark Vessey rising up, causing a lot of bloody upheavals.

So how did Negro comedians get into the blackface business? Well, in the beginning whites played the Jim Crow and Zip Coon roles; later, slaves forced to humor the master and amuse his family adopted them. Eventually, this created a number of professional Negro minstrels playing the coon as a means of survival and coexistence, much like the court jesters during Europe's troubador

age, who when they didn't please the king...
pow...off with their heads.

From 1850 to 1880, minstrelsy was the biggest
thing in U.S. theater. They called it the "Cullud
Opera," and famed actors like Edwin Booth and
Edwin Forrest toured the length and breadth of
the country, in effect proclaiming, "Here is what
the Negro is—lazy, shiftless, addicted to crap
games and watermelons." And they did this so
much until all reality concerning the Negro had to
conform to that description. Anyone who said it
wasn't so was considered nuts.

Much later during that era, Negro performers
began to enter minstrelsy in great numbers, and
the important thing about this was how we began
to change the comedy and the character of the
stump routines. Jokes like: "I just went to the
store and bought a pound of sugar for five dollars." "Well you're stupid paying five dollars for
a pound of sugar." "Stupid? Who's stupid? While
de white man was dishing up de sugar, I done
stole eight pair a shoes." So, you see, in this
context, stealing became a matter of survival, a
social comment, and these Negro satirists began
to slip in their own personal observations and the
dissatisfaction of the Negro comedian began to
color his act.

Bert Williams was the best example of this
kind of reverse lampoon. He bridged the gap
between minstrelsy and vaudeville and was by far
the best black comedian to come along till then.
He became so well known for the skillful comic
interpretations he was able to create within the

limitations of the "stage Negro" that he eventually became a star headliner in the Ziegfeld Follies
for some ten years.

You can't talk about vaudeville unless you
mention Bert Williams. He was that great. There
must be hundreds of stories in show business
about him. There is a classic about Williams'
going into a bar on Broadway, right next to the
Ziegfeld Theater where he was pulling down
$4,000 a week. He walked into the bar with two
white theatrical people but the barman was about
to refuse to serve him. "All right, I'll have three
scotches," Williams said. "That'll be $100 for
you," the bartender said. And Williams went . . .
"Pht, pht, pht," and peeled off $300 and said,
"There it is. Now give me my three scotches."

That was the breed of man Williams was and
the story should give you some idea of the environment black comedians had to exist in during
those early days. With no alternative positions
open in entertainment, the great black humorists
of the past made money and survived off of the
"Negro stage role" as given, changing it with the
best weapon they had—implacable and tenacious
talent. Bert Williams grinning and rolling his
eyes, singing *Nobody,* the song he helped make
famous, was always protest, and he literally
sang . . . "When I was in that engine wreck, who
was it took that engine off my neck? Nobody.
And I ain't going to do nothing for nobody till
somebody does something for me."

Usually when people ask, "Godfrey, what comedian of the past do you admire?" most likely I
answer, "Bert Williams." And then you get a

surprise reply about, "Oh! He was a blackface comedian." Now right in here I say a bit about, "But for the grace of God goes you know who," because Williams paved the path away from blackface with his professionalism during a time when the ability of Negroes to draw big-time box office had to be proved. Actually, without making a grandstand apology, when something is outstanding all you can do is admire it, no matter what form it's in, which is exactly what white comedians did about Bert Williams.

The history of vaudeville in America is the history of a lot of admiration and a lot of bootlegging going on around Bert Williams. It was a typical demonstration of Langston Hughes' phrase, "They done took our blues and gone," because white performers took the rudiments of Williams' act and stylized them into highly successful formulas. This was the case with another Negro act called Butterbeans and Suzie. Butterbeans originated the routine about the guy with the dumb wife who is always being bugged by her, and this later got translated as George Burns and Gracie Allen. So in its way, vaudeville summed up was the Ossie Davis remark from *Purlie Victorious,* when he said, "Somebody has got to help me, because, look at that, two white men put black cork on their faces and went out as Amos and Andy and made a million dollars. And here I am, born with the stuff, and can't earn a dime."

> "... he became a hero ... because
> he was saying things that everyone
> thought but never said."

Well, the parade of white performers who ben-
efited from all this bootlegging is, you know . . . Al
Jolson, Eddie Cantor, Ted Lewis and too many
minor stars to mention. Meanwhile, during the
Jolson era, black performers had to take what
they could, some of them fortunately enough
creating work for themselves through the growth
of Negro revues that came into popularity during
the '20s. People like Ethel Waters, Pigmeat
Markham and even Moms Mabley started in these
"shuffle-along" type "Cotton Club" revues. They
called it the Negro renaissance because it meant
that a lot of black performers were working steady,
maybe for the first time.

Now, at the moment when black comedians
were trying desperately to break away from blackface altogether, there was on the other hand a
reissue of the servile Uncle Tom image in films
of the late 1920s and '30s. This resurgence of
Tomism in cinema came at a time when Klan
lynchings were numerous, when Negro civil rights
organizations were beginning to materialize, and
when race riots between blacks and immigrants
were frequent. So once again the comic Negro
became white society's release of tension. For
this reason, Hollywood felt the need to project an
image of the black as someone from whom white
audiences would have nothing to fear. We were
stuck with the minstrel image again, this time
without the blackface disguise.

The presentation of this stereotype usually broke
down into two distinguishing acting formulas.
There was the Charlie Chan school and the schoolteacher school.

In the Charlie Chan school everything was ghosts. Negroes were afraid of ghosts and anything spooky, and they were always childlike and simple, and there was Stepin Fetchit and Mantan Moreland and Willie Best. They were always housemen or gardeners and they never had any love life—or if they did it was always a kind of cute kitchen table romance with the next-door maid, and of course they never got married. Mostly, though, they were afraid of ghosts.

In the schoolteacher characterization, there were Hattie McDaniel and Bill Robinson. They used to play in all those Shirley Temple movies and Bill Robinson would always teach Shirley how to dance. Negroes were always teachers in that era: I remember one picture, *Birth of the Blues,* when Mary Martin said to Rochester, "Rochester, would you teach me—teach me how to sing like colored people?" I will always remember that line because it is typical of the ridiculous kind of unreality the black comedian was forced to participate in at that time.

Emancipation for the black comic from the setback caused by Hollywood's reissue of the minstrel stereotype did not begin until around 1940. What was taking place, of course, was the migration of the blacks to the city, to the great urban areas of Chicago, New York, Baltimore and Washington. Concurrently, this gave rise to an outbreak of the black vaudeville houses and the black vaudeville circuit, theaters with movies produced for these audiences.

There was Ralph Cooper, one of the great stars of the all-black films. There were black gangsters, black cops, black good guys, and chases on 125th Street to the Harlem River to get the bad guys. It was a world in which white people did not exist, and at least here at last was a kind of equal world.

And for the first time you had sort of a male hero image in these features. Take any major black neighborhood and you would find these pictures, playing at places like the Regent in Brooklyn or the Apollo in Harlem. They were not great, these Grade-B movies, but they did project a positive image for the first time in American theatrical history. Somehow the black kid could say, "Gee whiz, I can get back at somebody if they bug me, 'cause Ralph Cooper did it." And they got a new insight into themselves. So it was here in these Grade-B movie houses that a new black comedian began to flourish.

As always, after the picture the variety show would come on and you would have a master of ceremonies who addressed you as "Ladies and Gentlemen" and who wore great clothes, no more baggy pants. And this MC, who was a comic, had jokes that were sharp and witty, jokes that put down man, put down government, talked about the South and North, talked about our living conditions, the landlord, Father Divine; yes sir-ree, that even ridiculed holy personages with a kind of biting irreverence.

In these routines, this home-brewed breed like Timmie Rogers, Alan Drew, Nipsey Russell, Redd Foxx and Slappy White were speaking more and more the common inside humor of the streets. They became pungent social voices. Consequently, for the first time a black comedian became a hero, he became a hero of the entire community because he was saying things that everyone thought about but never said.

With veteran performers like this, all of a sudden there was no more shuffle, all of a sudden with Timmie, Nipsey, Slappy or Redd there was someone to identify with. You might be in the Uptown Theater in Philadelphia or the Tivoli and Regal in Chicago or the Royal in Baltimore and these cats would come on stage standing up tall and straight, looking you in the eye, saying what they had to say. They might perhaps be wearing a weskit or a Brooks Brothers' suit, and you'd say, "Wow, oh baby, dig the vines on that cat. Man, oh Lord, I got to get me a tail like that."

Well now, that was the history and all of this brings us pretty much around to present cases and pretty much proves my point . . . how without the ground-breaking image projected by the comics of the Negro vaudeville circuit, without the attempts to break the Jim Crow stereotype by black entertainers in the minstrel past, the breakthrough into the white big time that has taken place for Dick Gregory, Bill Cosby, Nipsey Russell, George Kirby and myself would never have happened.

Why things are clarifying themselves so fast, every time you turn on the TV you see one of us hotshots commenting on the government, and now with Bill Cosby co-starring as a network television serial star, there's no telling. . . . Why one day you'll switch on the channel and see one of us lounging around on that TV screen in our pajamas like Jack Benny, and pretty soon things are going to get so good we won't be Negro comics at all.

I can just imagine flying over to Hollywood for a film-casting session, one of those African spectaculars where you wear a loin cloth and a bone stuck in your hair, and the producer saying . . . how he didn't have me in mind for that part at all, and would I consider playing Suzie Wong's father in the interest of racial progress. And I can just see myself giving him that loud, boisterous dressing down us people are supposed to be famous for. "Man," I'll say, "you must be kidding, I ain't about to lose my complete identity just to get a job from you people."

By Godfrey Cambridge, from *Tuesday* magazine, W. Leonard Evans, Jr., President and Publisher.

Answers: **1.** _____

_____

2. _____

_____

3. _____

_____

Review

Since reading is a thinking process, not an exercise in eye movement, mastering this part of the communication process requires a series of skills. To be useful, the skills must have a logical sequence that can become habitual, automatic.

1st—**Set a purpose**, a reason for reading, by asking, "Why am I reading this?"

Use the six questions to guide you:
What? Who? When? Where? How? Why?

2nd—**Speculate** on what the answers will be. Get involved. Set up your own mental challenge based on your own past experience and what you already know.

3rd—**Select** the method of reading that will most efficiently satisfy your purpose, answer the question you want answered:

Skim-Type reading that you've been practicing, **scan-type reading** or **study-type reading** that you're about to learn.

You may find that one former participant expressed how you feel at this point in the program. He said the course so far reminded him of the period when he gave up his tricycle and learned to ride his first bicycle. Like trying to manage the new, large bike, **setting purpose questions** and **speculating** were awkward and slowed him down. He doubted their value.

But when he practiced until the new skills became second nature—both with the new bike and the new reading skills— he enjoyed a wonderful new command of part of his world for the rest of his life.

With practice, you can know the same success.

Scan-Type Reading

Second Level of Comprehension— Interpretation of Meanings

Let's begin by defining **scan-type reading.**

> **Scan-type reading** is a quick, orderly search for the author's statements that will answer your purpose questions *How?* and *Why?*

Scanning requires accurate identification of the author's statements of *how* or *why* something happened. You **skim** the article looking for key words, possibly matching words, that are part of your **purpose question.** You want to recognize a sequence of events, a series of numbered points, or a general order of ideas. You search for reasons that will produce more details and be more qualifying than just the facts that answer **skim-type** questions.

Scan-type reading is slower than **skimming**. You are usually reading for more than one-word answers, and the specific information may be scattered throughout the selection. Both discrimination and interpretation are used to select the facts that answer *your* questions. Rather than just the author's direct answers, you may need to interpret statements (ideas) that can create relationships between facts, time sequences, generalizations, definitions, or values.

You may need to identify cause-and-effect relationships or related categories of ideas that have common characteristics. Your question may lead you to identify a reason, then find other examples related to that reason or draw conclusions from information learned by reading graphs, charts, or tables of statistics.

Begin your practice with Exercise 19. Use our question as your purpose for **scan**-reading the article. Then **speculate** on the answer to the **purpose question** before you **scan**-read for the correct answer to write after the article.

E X E R C I S E   1 9

Our Question: How do long-range factors affect com-
                  modity prices?
Our Speculation: They force prices up.
Your Speculation: _____

You want to begin by finding where the discussion of long-range factors begins and where it ends. Look for "long-range factors." Then you know your answer is in that section of the article.

Commodity Price Movements

Factors that affect price are both long- and short-range. Consider the long-range first. The price of any single commodity is bound to be influenced by the general level of all commodity prices. There are periods of gradual rises and periods of slowly sinking prices. From 1866 to 1893 commodity prices were in a slow decline. From 1893 until World War I there was an advancing level. Commodity prices prior to World War II were relatively low. After World War II there was a rise. In 1953 another descending trend began.

We must be aware of the price trend of all commodities in order to study one or two. A number of indices register prices—the Bureau of Labor Statistics, Dow Jones, and an index by the Commodity Research Bureau of commodities traded on futures exchanges. Using the proper index gives the correct picture of what is happening in various groups of commodities.

Another long-range factor is the value of money. Any change naturally affects commodity price levels. As money declines in value, commodity prices tend to rise; more money has to be used to make a purchase because the intrinsic value of the commodity itself has not changed. People have "hedged" by exchanging their money for something with more stability.

A change in a foreign exchange rate may cause the volume of exports or imports to vary.

Population increase is a factor—the greater demand for goods bolsters prices.

Government price activity has tremendous long-range effects. We have had farm price support programs of some sort since the 1930's.

Then there is diminishing cost of production. Changes take place—new methods of transporting, new agricultural techniques—tending to reduce the price of the final produce.

This briefly covers some long-range factors affecting commodity prices.

But most daily activity at the Chicago Board of Trade concerns itself with short-range factors. For instance, the short-term trader will be very concerned about weather, insect damage, and so on, that might affect the supply of a crop being traded right now. Price rises when the crop is small, but this would only last until a normal crop is produced or to the point that another commodity can be economically substituted for the one in short supply.

Reprinted from *Marketing Grain*, Chicago Board of Trade.

Answer: _____
_____
_____

EXERCISE 20

Proceed with this article, **scanning** and answering the questions after you **speculate** on the answers.

Our Question: **1.** Why did the House fall?
Your Speculation: _____

Our Question: **2.** Why was J. P. Morgan called the King of Credit?
Your Speculation: _____

The Fall of the House of Morgan

A black, torpedo-shaped cigar belches smoke from beneath an awesome red nose, and two belligerent eyes glare fiercely across the stretch of years. It is John Pierpont (Jupiter Pluvius) Morgan. J. P. Morgan did more to shape the course of American industry since the turn of the century than any other man. Yet, paradoxically, his firm itself has just about dropped from sight, surviving only as the "Morgan" in Morgan Guaranty Trust Co. and in Morgan, Stanley & Co.

A company is fundamentally an idea. But the idea needs money for its potential to become actual. More often than not, the hand turning the faucet of American equity capital during the formative period of today's great corporations belonged to J. P. Morgan. Among the great Morgan-financed companies: AT&T, General Electric, International Harvester, Kennecott, the New York Central Railroad, the New Haven, the Northern Pacific, Pullman, the Southern Railway, U. S. Steel, Western Union, and Westinghouse Electric.

Morgan The Terrible, whose fierce gaze was compared to the headlight of the Cannonball Express bearing down upon you, was the undisputed captain of capital.

KING OF CREDIT

The nation became concerned that one man controlled its pocketbook. In 1912–13, Representative Arsene Pujo attacked the so-called "money trust" of Wall Street. Pujo showed that there were six key dispensers of credit in the country: J. P. Morgan & Co.; the First National Bank of New York; Kidder, Peabody & Co.; Lee Higginson & Co. and Kuhn, Loeb & Co. Morgan was by far the most powerful of the six, even though it was only the twelfth-largest investment banking house.

The Pujo investigation further showed that Morgan and his partners had deposits totaling $162 million; that Morgan had a powerful voice in banks with resources of $723 million; that he himself owned 51% of the $500 million Equitable Life Assurance Society; and that—in sum—he could put his hands on about $1.4 billion worth of liquid assets at a moment's notice.

In terms of influence, Morgan's power looked even more awesome. He and his partners held 72 directorships and controlled both the Banker's Trust and the Guaranty Trust. When linked with his traditional allies, the First National Bank and the National City Bank, the number of directorships influenced by J. P. Morgan jumped to 341. On top of this huge pyramid of power sat great "Jupiter Pluvius" himself, with an estimated 25% controlling interest in J. P. Morgan & Co.

The first curb on Morgan's powers came in 1902. As he sat at dinner one night he was informed that the Attorney General was preparing to file an antitrust suit against Morgan's Northern Securities Co. Deeply concerned, Morgan quickly journeyed down to Washington to protest that President Roosevelt could have given him advance warning. "Send your man to my man and they can fix it up," said Morgan, suggesting that the Attorney General of the U.S. meet with the attorney of J. P. Morgan & Co. After Morgan had departed, Roosevelt turned to the Attorney General and observed wryly: "Mr. Morgan could not help regarding me as a big rival operator." Two years later, Northern Securities was broken up.

Morgan had but to speak and millions of dollars flowed his way. In the middle of the 1907 panic, Morgan telephoned Charles A. Coffin, head of General Electric. "How much money have you

got?'' Morgan asked. Coffin proudly assured
Morgan that General Electric could weather the
storm with little difficulty. ''How much?'' Morgan
repeated. ''Fifteen million in cash,'' came the
reply. ''Send half of it over at once,'' Morgan
growled and hung up. It was the beginning of the
great capital pool that supported the market in
1907.

But today the great House of Morgan is only a
pale shadow of what it once was in terms of
power and influence. Split in two by the Glass-
Steagall Act of 1933, which forbade all banks
with Federal Reserve affiliation to be closely affil-
iated with brokerage houses, it is now a commercial bank, the Morgan Guaranty Trust Co., and a
conservative investment house, Morgan, Stanley
& Co.

In many ways, the imperious J. P. Morgan
sowed the seeds of his own destruction, just as
many a corporate chief executive has done. His
successful financings were largely the result of
combination, usually through horizontal integration. They were not particularly creative. Rarely
did they back a technological advance in its infan-
cy. Morgan's impulse was to regiment what already existed rather than to create new businesses.
Once Morgan backed Thomas A. Edison's electric light experiments, but soon broke with Edison.
Morgan was convinced that the idea had only
limited appeal to corporations and a wealthy few;
he refused to back Edison with any more funds
and even made him pay for the use of his own
patent.

Morgan also stubbed his august toes on various

projects because his one thought, horizontal integration, was not the universal panacea he thought it was. The ill-fated International Mercantile Marine venture was a case in point.

It might also be said of Morgan that he failed to develop management that would be able to take over when he died. His son John Pierpont, Jr. (Jack), who took over as titular head of the firm when Morgan died in 1913, was ill-prepared for the task. A product of St. Paul's and Harvard, Jack lived the life of an upperclass Englishman until the age of 40. Trained in the English branch of the firm, he was shy and self-effacing and neither able nor inclined to be the leader his father had been. Able Thomas W. Lamont and Henry P. Davidson made the key decisions.

But the Pujo Committee was just the beginning of the problems the House of Morgan had to face. With the first Democratic administration in 20 years installed in 1913, the world became vastly more complicated. First there was the 16th Amendment giving Congress the power to tax income; then the Physical Valuation Act, which led to railroad rate control; then the Federal Reserve Act; then the Federal Trade Commission Act, which gave the FTC the right to demand reports from corporations; and finally there was the Clayton Antitrust Act.

Instead of trying to come up with a new approach to backing corporations, the Morgan firm turned more and more to the field of international finance, in effect trying to refinance countries the way his father had refinanced railroads. It wasn't nearly as profitable.

THE TEST

When the crisis of 1929 came, Jack Morgan just couldn't do what his father had done in 1907. Not only was it a far deeper, more complex crisis, but also the lines of power and authority linking the House of Morgan with the business community and its coffers had weakened considerably.

A bitter public turned on the House of Morgan in 1933 as a scapegoat for the Depression, and Congress split the old firm in two with the Glass-Steagall Act of 1933.

It was the end of an era. Never again would any investment banker wield the power J. P. Morgan had wielded. But it is interesting to ponder how different the course of American industry might have been had Jack Morgan found that new way of using the Morgan power. Would the crash of 1929 have been so severe? One can almost see old Jupiter Pluvius shaking his hoary head.

Reprinted with permission from *Forbes*,
50th Anniversary Issue.

Answers: **1.** _____
          _____
          _____

Answers: **2.** _____
          _____
          _____

E X E R C I S E 2 1

Remember, don't let technical vocabulary or a crowded format distract you from your *purpose* for reading. Concentrate on the author's organization of thoughts that can help you find the answers you seek.

Our Question: What good trading principles can a speculator use?

Your Speculation: _____

Speculation and Speculators

The overwhelming majority of commodity speculators are position traders. They may be business and professional men, farmers or commodity handlers, to name some. All of them must have available capital, over and above their ordinary requirements, for venture purposes.

These people take long (buy) or short (sell) positions in the futures markets because they have formed an opinion that prices are about to advance or to decline. They derive their opinions of the market in a number of ways, but those who are consistently successful base their activities on a close study of fundamental market conditions plus a knowledge of trading techniques, two factors of equal importance.

Some of the most successful speculators are wrong in their market opinions more often than they are right. When they are wrong, they take losses quickly without having added new trades to their position. When they are right, however, they will pyramid their profitable trading experience so final over-all results are satisfactory.

Since there are nearly as many philosophies of trading in commodities as there are individual traders, it is virtually impossible to lay down any hard fast rules. However, out of experience certain trading principles have emerged that merit serious consideration. Here are some of the best:

1. Have a definite plan. Don't act on impulse and don't allow the original plan to be upset by temporary developments; but be sure you're in step with the market before asserting your position.
2. Don't over-trade. Always hold some funds in reserve.
3. Limit losses and allow profits to run. Most successful traders find that the failure to limit losses and the urge to take small profits quickly would be their downfall.
4. Learn all you can about the commodity being traded. Be guided by fundamental economic forces and common sense, not by fragmentary information or "hot tips."

It helps to understand how to trade, to pyramid a position, how and where to enter stop-loss orders, how to gather useful information from a chart, how to interpret published statistics in order to learn about the internal structure of the market. This information, whether fundamental or technical, is used to choose market situations that appear low in risk in relation to profit potentials.

Even though we have broken speculation into three categories, all are basically united in what they perform for our economy. The position trader takes a long-term risk; the scalper makes for second-to-second fluidity in pit trade; the spreader helps to keep price differences in line—but all really contribute to the liquidity of contract markets.

Commodity speculation is not an easy way to get rich quick. One professional describes speculation as a very hard way to make an easy living. Commodity speculation, like any other business, demands certain characteristics of the successful operator—intelligence, courage, knowledge, prudence, alertness. These are characteristics of leadership in every segment of American business.

Reprinted from *Marketing Grain*, Chicago Board of Trade.

Answer: _____
_____
_____
_____

EXERCISE 22

Our Question: **1.** How was the metric system developed?
Your Speculation: _____

Our Question: **2.** Why is the word *meter* used?
Your Speculation: _____

Brief History of
Measurement Systems

*"Weights and measures may be ranked among the
necessaries of life to every individual of human
society. They enter into the economical arrangements
and daily concerns of every family. They are
necessary to every occupation of human industry: to
the distribution and security of every species of
property; to every transaction of trade and commerce;
to the labors of husbandman; to the ingenuity of
the artificer; to the studies of the philosopher; to the
researches of the antiquarian, to the navigation
of the mariner, and the marches of the soldier; to all
the exchanges of peace, and all the operations
of war. The knowledge of them, as in established use,
is among the first elements of education, and is
often learned by those who learn nothing else, not even
to read and write. This knowledge is riveted in
the memory by the habitual application of it to the
employments of men throughout life."*

John Quincy Adams
Report to the Congress, 1821.

Weights and measures were among the earliest
tools invented by man. Primitive societies needed
rudimentary measures for many tasks: constructing
dwellings of an appropriate size and shape,
fashioning clothing, or bartering food or raw
materials.

Man understandably turned first to parts of his body and his natural surroundings for measuring instruments. Early Babylonian and Egyptian records and the Bible indicate that length was first measured with the forearm, hand, or finger and that time was measured by the periods of sun, moon, and other heavenly bodies. When it was necessary to compare the capacities of containers such as gourds or clay or metal vessels, they were filled with plant seeds which were then counted to measure the volumes. When means for weighing were invented, seeds and stones served as standards. For instance, the "carat," still used as a unit for gems, was derived from the carob seed.

As societies evolved, weights and measures became more complex. The invention of numbering systems and the science of mathematics made it possible to create whole systems of weights and measures suited to trade and commerce, land division, taxation, or scientific research. For these more sophisticated uses it was necessary not only to weigh and measure more complex things—it was also necessary to do it accurately time after time and in different places. However, with limited international exchange of goods and communication of ideas, it is not surprising that different systems for the same purpose developed and became established in different parts of the world—even in different parts of a single continent.

THE ENGLISH SYSTEM

The measurement system commonly used in the United States today is nearly the same as that brought by the colonists from England. These measures had their origins in a variety of cultures—Babylonian, Egyptian, Roman, Anglo-Saxon, and Norman French. The ancient "digit," "palm," "span," and "cubit" units evolved into the "inch," "foot," and "yard" through a complicated transformation not yet fully understood.

Roman contributions include the use of the number 12 as a base (our foot is divided into 12 inches) and words from which we derive many of our present weights and measures names. For example, the 12 divisions of the Roman "pes," or foot, were called *unciae*. Our words "inch" and "ounce" are both derived from that Latin word.

The "yard" as a measure of length can be traced back to the early Saxon kings. They wore a sash or girdle around the waist—that could be removed and used as a convenient measuring device. Thus the word "yard" comes from the Saxon word "gird" meaning the circumference of a person's waist.

Standardization of the various units and their combinations into a loosely related system of weights and measures sometimes occurred in fascinating ways. Tradition holds that King Henry I decreed that the yard should be the distance from the tip of his nose to the end of his thumb. The length of a furlong (or furrow-long) was established by the early Tudor rulers as 220 yards. This led Queen Elizabeth I to declare, in the 16th century, that henceforth the traditional Roman mile of 5,000 feet would be replaced by one of 5,280 feet, making the mile exactly 8 furlongs and providing a convenient relationship between two previously ill-related measures.

Thus, through royal edicts, England by the 18th century had achieved a greater degree of standardization than the continental countries. The English units were well suited to commerce and trade because they had been developed and refined to meet commercial needs. Through colonization and dominance of world commerce during the 17th, 18th, and 19th centuries, the English system of weights and measures was spread to and established in many parts of the world, including the American colonies.

However, standards still differed to an extent undesirable for commerce among the 13 colonies. The need for greater uniformity led to clauses in the Articles of Confederation (ratified by the original colonies in 1781) and the Constitution of the United States (ratified in 1790) giving power to the Congress to fix uniform standards for weights and measures. Today, standards supplied to all the states by the National Bureau of Standards assure uniformity throughout the country.

THE METRIC SYSTEM

The need for a single worldwide coordinated measurement system was recognized over 300 years ago. Gabriel Mouton, Vicar of St. Paul in Lyons, proposed in 1670 a comprehensive decimal measurement system based on the length of one minute of arc of a great circle of the earth. In 1671 Jean Picard, a French astronomer, proposed the length of a pendulum beating seconds as the unit of length. (Such a pendulum would have been fairly easily reproducible, thus facilitating the widespread distribution of uniform standards.) Other proposals were made, but over a century elapsed before any action was taken.

In 1790, in the midst of the French Revolution, the National Assembly of France requested the French Academy of Sciences to "deduce an invariable standard for all the measures and all the weights." The Commission appointed by the academy created a system that was, at once, simple and scientific. The unit of length was to be a portion of the earth's circumference. Measures for capacity (volume) and mass (weight) were to be derived from the unit of length, thus relating the basic unit of the system to each other and to nature. Furthermore, the larger and smaller versions of each unit were to be created by multiplying or dividing the basic units by 10 and its powers. This feature provided a great convenience to users of the system, by eliminating the need for such calculations as dividing by 16 (to convert ounces to pounds) or by 12 (to convert inches to feet). Similar calculations in the metric system could be performed simply by shifting the decimal point. Thus the metric system is a "base-10" or "decimal" system.

The Commission assigned the name *metre*— which we spell meter—to the unit of length. This name was derived from the Greek word *metron,* meaning "a measure." The physical standard representing the meter was to be constructed so that it would equal one ten-millionth of the distance from the North Pole to the equator along the meridian of the earth running near Dunkirk in France and Barcelona in Spain.

The metric unit of mass, called the "gram," was defined as the mass of one cubic centimeter (a cube 1/100 of a meter on each side) of water at its temperature of maximum density. The cubic decimeter (a cube 1/10 of a meter on each side) was chosen as the unit of fluid capacity. This measure was given the name "liter."

Although the metric system was not accepted with enthusiasm at first, adoption by other nations occurred steadily after France made its use compulsory in 1840. The standardized character and decimal features of the metric system made it well suited to scientific and engineering work. Consequently, it is not surprising that the rapid spread of the system coincided with an age of rapid technological development. In the United States, by Act of Congress in 1866, it was made "lawful throughout the United States of America to employ the weights and measures of the metric system in all contracts, dealings or court proceedings."

By the late 1860's, even better metric standards were needed to keep pace with scientific advances. In 1875, an international treaty, the "Treaty of the Meter," set up well-defined metric standards for length and mass, and established permanent machinery to recommend and adopt further refinements in the metric system. This treaty, known as the Metric Convention, was signed by 17 countries, including the United States.

By 1900 a total of 35 nations—including the major nations of continental Europe and most of

South America—had officially accepted the metric system. Today, with the exception of the United States and a few small countries, the entire world is using predominantly the metric system or is committed to such use. In 1971 the Secretary of Commerce, in transmitting to Congress the results of a 3-year study authorized by the Metric Study Act of 1968, recommended that the U.S. change to predominant use of the metric system through a coordinated national program.

The International Bureau of Weights and Measures located in Sèvres, France, serves as a permanent secretariat for the Meter Convention, coordinating the exchange of information about the use and refinement of the metric system. As measurement science develops more precise and easily reproducible ways of defining the measurement units, the General Conference on Weights and Measures—the diplomatic organization made up of adherents to the Convention—meets periodically to ratify improvements in the system and the standards.

In 1960, the General Conference adopted an extensive revision and simplification of the system. The name *Le Système International d'Unités* (International System of Units), with the international abbreviation SI, was adopted for this modernized metric system.

Reprinted from U.S. Department of Commerce, National Bureau of Standards.

Answers: **1.** _____
_____
_____

Answers: **2.** _____
_____

EXERCISE 23

Our Question: **1.** Why is harvesting sphagnum peat moss
dependent on the weather?
Your Speculation: _____
_____

Our Question: **2.** Why are there concentrations of sphagnum peat moss in some areas?
Your Speculation: _____
_____

Our Question: **3.** How is sphagnum peat moss used?
Your Speculation: _____
_____

From Bog to Bale to Bench—
A Tale of Sphagnum Peat Moss

by Ann Reilly

What is this thing called peat moss, anyway?
Any grower worth his cuttings knows the advantages of using sphagnum peat moss in germinat-
ing or growing mixes: It is essentially sterile; it
provides good aeration; it is light; it has a predict-
able pH (3.5 to 4.5); it has a water-holding
capacity 12 to 20 times its weight; it is free from
harmful salts, chemicals or insects; it is 95 percent organic in nature, and it has a great capacity
to exchange ions. Many growers take peat moss
for granted and don't realize that this vital part of
our growing operation is the partially decomposed
fibrous root system of the sphagnum moss plant,
well known by basket growers as a lining material.

In addition to taking sphagnum peat moss for
granted, many growers are confused by its proper
name. Sphagnum moss, the basket liner, is only
one of many types of moss. The word "peat"
refers to partially decomposed vegetation, and so
"sphagnum peat moss" (actually, I think it would
make more sense to call the substance sphagnum
moss peat) refers to partially decomposed roots of
the sphagnum moss plant. Sphagnum should not
be confused with other types of mosses or other
types of peat—reed peat, sedge peat or Michigan
peat; unfortunately, it is. We have a tendency to
shorten the full name to just "peat" or "peat
moss." Only sphagnum peat moss, because of its

strong cellular structure, retains a high moisture-holding capacity even after decomposition. Sphagnum moss itself comes in 27 varieties, many of which are not suited for mechanical harvesting.

Before sphagnum peat moss is harvested, the trees are cleared (this isn't difficult because tree growth is spindly in pure peat), other brush is removed and then a drainage ditch is dug around the area.

The nature of sphagnum peat moss harvesting makes it totally dependent on the weather. Until about a dozen years ago, sphagnum peat moss was cut by hand into blocks, lifted from the bogs and stacked to dry. Since then, new methods of harvesting have been developed, and today, peat moss is harvested dry, vacuumed off the bogs.

Sphagnum peat moss bogs, which are divided into sections 750 feet wide and one mile long to accommodate the harvesting machinery, must be totally dry for a day or two before they are harrowed to rough up the surface to a depth of two inches. On the day after harrowing, machines resembling oil drums that have sprouted heating ducts are pulled across the bogs by tractors. The top layer of wind- and sun-dried peat is vacuumed off and stored in the drums, which are 10 feet long, eight feet in diameter and hold 14 cubic yards of peat moss. If the weather remains cooperative, the bogs are vacuumed again the next day, and so on. During an average year, two inches of sphagnum peat moss are removed.

After the peat is harvested by the vacuums and lined up in combine formation, it is piled high down the bogs to await transport in wagons into the plant. During this time, its moisture levels off until it approaches the ideal of 35 percent. When the sphagnum peat moss gets into the processing plant (which may be many months later), it is screened to remove sticks, roots and hard chunks. It is then sized for uniformity and then ground—if necessary. Sometimes it is turned into soilless mix with vermiculite, perlite, lime and fertilizer. Then it's baled into four- or six-cubic-yard bales. Throughout the entire process, the sphagnum peat moss is handled as gently as possible so the final product doesn't become so fine that it will produce aeration problems when it's put to work.

Peat producers sometimes worry about the converse of too much rain—too little, which heightens the chance of fire. Remember, dried peat is used as a fuel in many northern countries. A fire in a bog is very difficult to extinguish, especially in a strong wind. For this reason, no gasoline engines are allowed near the bog, and the drainage ditches are used not to carry water off but to hold it so the peat may be kept damp when the weather is very dry.

As peat moss is removed and the new tree roots are exposed, the bog is disced again and again. Weeds, too, create a problem—not on the bog but in the drainage ditches. Because of the possible contamination of the sphagnum peat moss, herbicides are not allowed on the property, so weed removal is mechanical and tedious.

It has been only during the last century that growers have realized the horticultural value of sphagnum peat moss, but the Irish, Scots, Germans and Russians have been burning sphagnum peat as fuel for ages. In some areas of the Soviet Union, peat is still used for fuel—and fuel only; although the USSR is the world's largest producer of peat moss, not one ounce ever sees the inside of a Soviet greenhouse. Canada is the principal supplier of sphagnum peat moss to the US: It exports an average of 400,000 tons to its southern neighbor each year.

Why are there concentrations of sphagnum peat moss in Canada, Russia, Ireland, Scotland and Germany? The climate of these countries and their geography are conducive to the growth of peat. Bogs are located in flat, low-lying areas roughly between the 46th and 55th parallels, where warm summers promote growth of the green moss and severe winters prevent the roots from decomposing completely. The acidity of the roots themselves also assists in slowing the decomposition process.

Will the world ever run out of sphagnum peat moss? Although the supply isn't endless, bogs are plentiful. The problem is that most of them are in remote areas. Even the youngest bog is five or six feet deep; if two inches are harvested each year, the bog will last at least 30 years. With bogs ranging in size from 1,000 to 2,500 acres, even the smallest bog can produce more than 250,000 cubic yards of peat per year. Sphagnum peat moss bogs are produced at the rate of one foot every 300 years; it's easy to calculate that the oldest bogs, which are as deep as 50 feet, began to form about 15,000 years ago.

HOW TO USE CANADIAN
SPHAGNUM PEAT MOSS

Sphagnum peat moss has a variety of uses both indoors and outside. For indoor gardening, it should be used with equal parts of soil and sand in pots, terrariums and dish gardens.

Sphagnum peat should be moistened before it is used. An easy way to do this is to lay the bale flat and cut a slit down the center, then across both ends, forming the letter "I." Open the flaps and pour a pail of warm water over the peat moss. Let it soak overnight. Add water from the garden hose next day if further moisture is desired. If you do not plan to use the entire bale immediately, store it in the shade, slightly off the ground and keep flaps closed when not in use. This will keep it sufficiently clean, but also moist.

NEW LAWNS

A two-inch layer of sphagnum peat moss should be worked into the top six inches of soil with a rototiller. Then seed, adding a ⅛-inch top dressing of sphagnum peat moss, and water thoroughly. The top dressing will hold the seeds in place, keep them moist during germination and protect them against extreme temperatures.

GARDENS

The success of a new garden depends on its soil structure. To assure a good growing medium in a new garden remove sod, stones and debris from the soil. Then work ample amounts of Canadian sphagnum peat moss into the soil. A six-cubic-foot bale of sphagnum peat moss for every 150 square feet of garden area is about right for average soil. If the soil is heavy in sand or clay, use double the amount of sphagnum peat.

Once the new garden has been started and is producing, the soil needs cannot be ignored from year-to-year. Tilling operations, walking on the surface and water percolating through the soil all increase compaction. Keep the soil structure fertile by spreading an inch layer of sphagnum peat moss over the entire garden area each year. Then work it into the top six inches with a garden tiller or spade.

SHRUBS AND TREES

Broad leaf evergreens, azaleas, camellias, rhododendrons, daphnes and heather are acid-loving plants. They need plenty of water, more air to root than any other plants, acid soil and good drainage. Sphagnum peat moss mixed with the soil provides all these needs whether you plant these evergreens outside or have them in pots or planters. They'll thrive if the roots are kept moist but not soggy. Though sphagnum peat moss holds many times its weight in water and keeps roots moist, it will always let excess water flow out.

Pines, spruces, junipers, yews, firs, arborvitae and other bushes and trees should be planted in soil mixed with equal parts of sphagnum peat moss. The soil should be soaked after planting and kept moist.

ROSES

Sandy or light soil should be mixed with equal parts of sphagnum peat moss to create an optimum growing medium for roses. If the soil is predominantly clay, a mixture of one-third soil and two-thirds sphagnum peat moss will provide an excellent base for these popular plants.

INDOOR GARDENS, POTTED PLANTS, HANGING BASKETS

Repotting Plants

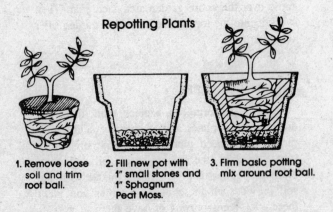

1. Remove loose soil and trim root ball.

2. Fill new pot with 1" small stones and 1" Sphagnum Peat Moss.

3. Firm basic potting mix around root ball.

The soil mix for indoor gardens should include at least one part sphagnum peat moss with other materials (potting soil and sand or vermiculite). For cacti and succulents, a double portion of sand is recommended. In all cases sphagnum peat moss retains moisture around plant roots, cutting down the frequency of watering and assuring that nutrients are easily available to the plants.

MULCHING

Because of its special structure, sphagnum peat moss is an excellent mulching material. Its insulating power and permeability means soil temperatures will be kept even, moisture loss through evaporation kept at a minimum and weeds eliminated. If sphagnum peat moss is used between rows of vegetables, it will keep them clean and free from soil-borne diseases.

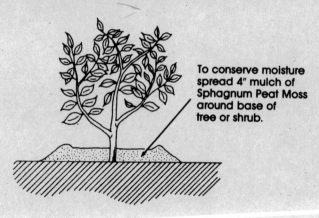

To conserve moisture spread 4" mulch of Sphagnum Peat Moss around base of tree or shrub.

Spread a two- to three-inch layer of sphagnum peat moss around the base of shrubs, trees and garden plants. Keep sphagnum peat moist. If dry spells are common in your area, mix equal amounts of grass clippings or shredded leaves with sphagnum peat moss before applying, to guard against crusting.

Canadian Sphagnum Peat Moss Information Bureau
Suite 634, Empire State Bldg.,
New York, NY 10001.

Answers: **1.** _____
_____

2. _____
_____

3. _____
_____

Study-Type Reading

Third Level of Comprehension— Creative Application

There are several differences in the reading-learning skills. One concerns your rate of reading:

> **Skim-type** reading is a rapid search for the author's few words that answer *What, Who, When, Where*. It is a simple one-step process of collecting information.

> **Scan-type** reading is a slower search for answers to *How* and *Why*. It is a two-step process involving collecting related facts and arranging them in a meaningful sequence.

> **Study-type** reading is the slowest, most deliberate type of reading to answer *How* and *Why*. It involves four steps:

1. *Gathering* facts and ideas.
2. *Sorting* facts and ideas for importance and relationships.
3. *Measuring* the ideas based on your experience and knowledge.
4. *Deciding* what you, the reader, will believe and want to remember and possibly act on, and what you cannot accept and want to reject.

It is apparent that we need all three types of reading to be a flexible, efficient reader. It is also understandable that your purpose for reading is essential for determining the appropriate type of reading to use for efficiency. Using the slower *study-type* reading for a task that could be accomplished by *skim-* or *scan-type* reading means poor time management.

Keeping the above summary in mind, let's define *study-type* reading:

Study-type reading is the most careful, in-depth type of reading that we do. It involves critical and analytical thinking to interpret, evaluate, judge, and categorize information and ideas that a writer presents.

We use **study-type** reading to answer implied instructions:

Explain . . . Describe . . . Evaluate . . .
Interpret . . . Illustrate . . . Define . . .
Compare . . . Tell the extent of . . . Account for . . .

The following exercises are selected to develop your **study-type** reading skill. Proceed as though the questions posed for each article are *your* questions, the ones you want answered. Use the **Question Words** to determine *How* and *Why* you will read the articles.

Study the questions, make them your own, and *keep them in mind while you read.*

Next, jot down your **speculations** to organize your knowledge of the subject.

Then read to find the answers to your questions—to verify your speculation or acquire new knowledge.

EXERCISE 24

Our Question: **1.** You are planning to drive your recreational vehicle to a Canadian national park for a fishing vacation. What arrangements must you make ahead of time?

Your Speculation: _____

_____

_____

Our Question: **2.** Using these two articles and your past experience, what would you find as the main attractions in the Canadian national parks?

Your Speculation: _____

_____

_____

Canada
Travel Information 1984
(for visitors from the U.S.A.)

ENTRY INTO CANADA

FROM THE UNITED STATES

Citizens or legal, permanent residents of the United States do not require passports or visas and can usually cross the U.S.A.–Canada border without difficulty or delay. However, to assist officers in speeding the crossing, and particularly to re-enter the U.S.A., native-born U.S. citizens should carry some identification papers showing their citizenship, such as a birth, baptismal or voter's certificate. Proof of residence may also be required. Naturalized U.S. citizens should carry a naturalization certificate or some other evidence of citizenship. Legal, permanent residents of the United States who are not U.S. citizens are advised to carry their Alien Registration Receipt Card (U.S. Form I-151 or Form I-551).

Persons under 18 years of age who are not accompanied by an adult should bring a letter from a parent or guardian giving them permission to travel to Canada.

FROM OTHER COUNTRIES

Citizens of the United States may enter Canada, as visitors, from any country without requiring a passport or visa. Legal, permanent residents of the United States do not require a passport or visa if they enter Canada from St. Pierre and

Miquelon. If they enter Canada from other countries, they do require passports. Also, visas are required unless they are citizens of a country that is visa exempt.

FROM OTHER COUNTRIES VIA THE UNITED STATES

All persons other than U.S. citizens or legal, permanent residents of the United States require a valid passport or an acceptable travel document. Some persons require a visa to enter Canada. Visitors should direct their enquiries regarding visa applications and valid travel documents to the Canadian Embassy or Consulate in their home country before departure for the United States. Only in emergency situations should applications be made to Canadian Consulates in the United States located in Atlanta, Boston, Buffalo, Chicago, Cleveland, Dallas, Detroit, Los Angeles, Minneapolis, New Orleans, New York City, Philadelphia, San Francisco and Seattle, or to the Canadian Embassy in Washington.

Visitors who wish to return to the United States after visiting Canada should check with an office of the U.S. Immigration and Naturalization Service to make sure they have all the necessary papers to get back into the United States.

Visitors under the transit-without-visa privilege must establish: that they are admissible to the U.S.A. under immigration laws; that they have confirmed onward reservations to Canada; that they will continue their journey on the same line or on a connecting line within eight hours after their arrival in the U.S.A. Such travellers cannot transfer to a connecting transportation line more than twice. The second form of transportation must depart for a foreign location (but not necessarily non-stop). The total period of waiting time for connecting transportation should never exceed eight hours, unless there is no scheduled transportation within the eight-hour period. In such a case, the traveller must continue his journey on the first available form of transportation.

EMPLOYMENT OR STUDY IN CANADA

Persons wishing to study or work in Canada must obtain a student or employment authorization before coming to Canada, except in certain cases specified by regulation. Citizens or legal, permanent residents of the United States, St. Pierre and Miquelon or Greenland may apply at a Canadian port of entry, but an authorization will only be granted if all the normal prerequisites have been fulfilled, including a medical examination and job clearance, where necessary. Employment authorizations are not issued if there are qualified Canadians or permanent residents available for the work in question. Persons wishing to work or study in Canada should contact the nearest Canadian Embassy or Consulate for further information.

ENTRY BY PRIVATE MOTOR VEHICLES

The entry of vehicles and vacation trailers into Canada for touring purposes is generally a quick and routine matter. Customs permits, if required, are issued at time of entry. Rental vehicles or trailers of the U-haul variety are also admissible. However, the vehicle registration forms should be carried together with a copy of the rental contract to indicate that use in Canada is authorized by the rental agency. Visitors entering Canada with vehicles not registered to themselves should also carry a letter from the owner to indicate that use of the vehicle is authorized.

VACATION TRAILERS

If you plan to leave your vacation trailer in Canada for a season while you return home from time to time, ask Canadian Customs for a wallet-sized special permit—an E-99. Post the permit inside the trailer so that it can be seen easily from outside.

There's no need to hand the permit back at the end of the season, but watch out for the expiry date. You may NOT store a vacation trailer in Canada during the off-season.

ENTRY BY PRIVATE AIRCRAFT

The entry of private tourist aircraft is generally a quick, routine matter. Visiting pilots should plan to land at an airport that can provide Customs clearance, must report to Canada Customs immediately and complete all documentation. In emergencies, visitors must report their arrival to the nearest regional Customs office or the nearest office of the Royal Canadian Mounted Police (RCMP).

For the convenience of visiting pilots, the publication *Air Tourist Information*—Canada (TP77IE) is available on request from:

Transport Canada
AISP/A
Ottawa, Ontario, Canada
K1A 0N8
Telephone: (613) 955-0197

ENTRY BY PRIVATE BOAT

Visitors planning to enter Canada by private boat should contact Customs in advance for a list of ports of entry that provide Customs facilities and their hours of operation. Immediately upon arrival, visitors must report to Customs and complete all documentation. In emergency situations, visitors must report their arrival to the nearest regional Customs office or office of the RCMP.

BRINGING GOODS INTO CANADA

PERSONAL BAGGAGE, RECREATIONAL EQUIPMENT

Visitors may bring into Canada certain goods as personal baggage, duty- and tax-free, provided all such items are declared to Canada Customs on arrival, and are not subject to restriction. Personal baggage may include such items as: fishing tackle, boats and motors, snowmobiles, etc.; equipment for camping, golf, tennis, scuba diving; radios, television sets, musical instruments, typewriters, cameras, and other items of a personal nature to be used in Canada during the visit. Consumable goods may also be included in the quantities listed below.

ALCOHOLIC BEVERAGES

If visitors meet the minimum age requirements of the province or territory of entry (19 years in British Columbia, New Brunswick, Newfoundland, Northwest Territories, Nova Scotia, Ontario, Saskatchewan and Yukon; 18 years in Alberta, Manitoba, Prince Edward Island and Quebec) they may bring into Canada, duty-free, either:

a) 1.1 litres (40-ounces) of liquor or wine; or

b) 24 336-ml (12-ounce) cans or bottles of beer or ale, or their equivalent of 8.2 litres (288 fl. ounces).

Additional quantities of alcoholic beverages— up to a maximum of 9 litres (2 gallons)—may be imported into Canada (except to Prince Edward Island and the Northwest Territories) on payment of duty and taxes, plus provincial fees at the port of entry.

TOBACCO PRODUCTS

Persons 16 years of age or over may bring into Canada, duty-free, 50 cigars, 200 cigarettes and 0.9 kg (2 pounds) of manufactured tobacco. Federal duty and taxes apply to additional quantities.

FOOD

Subject to the restrictions listed, up to two days' supply of food products per person may be imported without assessment. Quantities in excess of two days' supply may be imported on payment of duty at a rate of 17.5%, calculated on the value as expressed in Canadian dollars.

GASOLINE AND OIL

Gasoline and oil imported for consumption are dutiable. However, reasonable quantities for the tourist's use, for example gas and oil up to the normal capacity of the vehicle, are granted free entry.

SECURITY DEPOSIT REQUIREMENTS

As explained earlier, conveyances and personal goods may be imported temporarily into Canada by visitors for their own use without payment of duties or taxes. With the exception of consumable items or recreational equipment for which a seasonal permit has been obtained, all goods must be taken out of Canada at the conclusion of the visit. In some instances, it may be necessary for Customs to ensure that an item is re-exported and, for this purpose, a refundable security deposit is requested at the time of entry. The deposit is refunded to the visitor's home address after the item or items are taken out of Canada. A security deposit is normally a nominal amount, but may be as high as the amount of duty and tax which otherwise applies. However, as a general rule, Canada Customs does not require security deposits when travellers enter Canada with their goods solely for vacation or pleasure purposes.

GIFTS

Bona fide gifts may be sent to friends or relatives residing in Canada, or may be imported by visitors, duty- and tax-free, provided the value of each gift does not exceed $25 (Canadian funds), and the gifts do *not* consist of tobacco products, alcoholic beverages or advertising material. Gift packages sent by mail should be plainly marked "UNSOLICITED GIFT" and the value must be indicated.

Gifts valued at more than $25 (Canadian funds) will be subject to regular duty and taxes on the excess amount.

Note: Applicable rates for duty and taxes are available only from Canada Customs.

RETENTION OF BOATS AND MOTORS IN CANADA

Boats and motors, including boat trailers, may be retained in Canada beyond the period of normal use *only* if legitimate repairs and maintenance work are to be undertaken by a bona fide marina or service depot during the off-season. Under this procedure, the owner must provide Customs with a copy of the work order or a written statement from the individual or firm who will be effecting the repairs, indicating a description of the article, the name and address of the owner, the type of work to be done, and the time and location at which the work will be effected. Customs will issue a small blue form, called an "E-99," which must be affixed to the boat in a place where it will remain clearly visible. Units left in Canada during the off-season without benefit of this procedure are liable to seizure and forfeiture, unless duties and taxes have been paid.

TRANSPORTING GOODS THROUGH CANADA

From time to time, residents of the United States wish to transport personally their household or personal effects between one part of mainland U.S.A. and another—or Alaska—through Canada. In such instances, when the goods are not intended for use in Canada, they may be transported "intransit," under control of a temporary admission permit, form E29B. While no assessment is applicable, a refundable security deposit may be required at the time of entry.

Special restrictions apply to certain firearms.

To facilitate the intransit movement of goods through Canada, the traveller should prepare, in advance, a list of such goods in triplicate, indicating their respective values and serial numbers, where applicable. Consumable goods such as foodstuffs or alcoholic beverages which are intended for consumption outside may also be moved intransit, provided they are listed and packed in containers or packages that can be corded and sealed by Canada Customs at the time of entry.

SEASONAL RESIDENTS

Non-residents of Canada who inherit, are given, buy, build or rent (on a three-year lease or longer) a permanent structure in Canada for use as a seasonal residence (mobile or portable homes do not qualify), have a one-time privilege of furnishing the residence with certain kinds of goods free of duty. A brochure, *Seasonal Residents,* is available from Canada Customs and outlines the necessary requirements.

BRINGING ANIMALS, PLANTS AND FOOD INTO CANADA

The following information applies to non-commercial items a person might bring into Canada, for personal use, which originate from the United States.

All animals, plants, vegetables, fruit and meat, and any product of these items, must be declared to Canada Customs at the first port of entry into Canada, must be accompanied by import documentation when required, and must pass inspection.

PET ANIMALS AND BIRDS

Domestic dogs and cats may be imported from the United States provided each animal is accompanied by a certificate issued by a licensed veterinarian of Canada or the United States which clearly identifies the animal and certifies that the dog and/or cat has been vaccinated against rabies during the preceding 36-month period.

Puppies and kittens under three months of age and "seeing eye" dogs accompanied by their owner may enter Canada without certification or further restriction.

Up to two pet birds (birds of the parrot family and songbirds) per family may be imported into Canada provided: a) the owner accompanies the birds to Canada; b) the owner makes a declaration on arrival in Canada that certifies, for all of the 90 days preceding the date of entry, the birds have not been in contact with any other bird, or birds, and that they have been in the visitor's personal possession for this period.

A Canadian import permit and quarantine in Canada are required for the importation of more than two parrot-type birds from the United States. The import of more than two birds of any species from the United States is subject to a valid United States veterinary certificate accompanying the birds to Canada.

Pet monkeys and small pet mammals, fish and reptiles (other than turtles and tortoises), may enter Canada from the United States without certification or restriction.

Turtles and tortoises require a Canadian import permit before admission to Canada.

Pet foxes and skunks, raccoons and ferrets, as personal pets only, may be admitted to Canada without health certification or an import permit, provided they are accompanied by the owner.

OTHER ANIMALS

Any livestock, horses, wild or domestic fowl, or commercial shipment of animals including all species of birds, are subject to veterinary health inspection on arrival in Canada and may require the prior issuance of an import permit and/or United States export health certification.

Persons wishing to import such animals from the United States should enquire of the exact conditions necessary and should also contact the Food Production and Inspection Offices nearest to the intended port of entry to arrange for the inspection of the animals on their arrival.

ENDANGERED SPECIES

The importation of endangered species of animals and plants, and their products, is restricted and may require the prior issuance of an import permit. This restriction also applies to certain animal skins and mounted animals and trophies.

PLANTS, FRUIT AND VEGETABLES

House plants (plants commonly known and recognized as house plants grown or intended to be grown indoors, when carried as personal effects) will not require a "phytosanitary (plant health) certificate" to enter Canada from the continental U.S.A.

Vegetables from certain parts of the following states are restricted entry into Canada: Alabama, Arkansas, North and South Carolina, Delaware, Florida, Georgia, Illinois, Indiana, Iowa, Kentucky, Louisiana, Maryland, Minnesota, Mississippi, Missouri, New York, Oklahoma, Tennessee, Texas, and Virginia. Visitors from these states should contact their nearest office of the U.S. Department of Agriculture for more details.

As restrictions can vary on plants, fruits and vegetables, and are subject to change at short notice, visitors are advised to check in advance with the nearest office of the U.S. Department of Agriculture.

TAKING PLANTS OUT OF CANADA

Tourists may take plants of Canadian origin
(except certain prohibited items) into the United
States provided the plants are accompanied by a
''phytosanitary (plant health) certificate'' which
may be obtained from any Plant Products and
Quarantine Division Offices of Agriculture Canada, located in major centres across Canada.

*Government of Canada, Industry, Trade and Commerce
and Regional Economic Expansion.*

National Parks of Canada

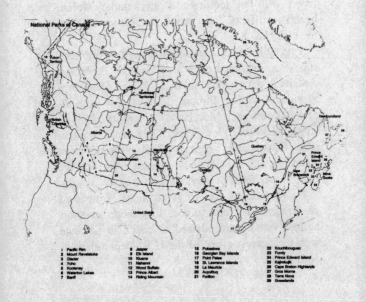

1 Pacific Rim	8 Jasper	15 Pukaskwa	22 Kouchibouguac
2 Mount Revelstoke	9 Elk Island	16 Georgian Bay Islands	23 Fundy
3 Glacier	10 Kluane	17 Point Pelee	24 Prince Edward Island
4 Yoho	11 Nahanni	18 St. Lawrence Islands	25 Kejimkujik
5 Kootenay	12 Wood Buffalo	19 La Mauricie	26 Cape Breton Highlands
6 Waterton Lakes	13 Prince Albert	20 Auyuittuq	27 Gros Morne
7 Banff	14 Riding Mountain	21 Forillon	28 Terra Nova
			29 Grasslands

NATIONAL PARKS OF CANADA

There is at least one national park in every province and territory: thirteen in Western Canada, six in Central Canada, seven in the Atlantic provinces, and three in the true North of the Yukon and Northwest Territories. The Trans-Canada Highway and other major roads provide access routes to most of Canada's twenty-nine national parks.

This guide will help you to pick the national park that offers the kind of outdoor experience you are seeking. Whether you are a trailer camper or a backpacker, a bird-watcher or mountain climber, there is a national park to suit your appetite for the great outdoors. On the following pages you will learn more about the national parks and what makes each one different from all the rest.

The national parks have been set aside so that Canadians will always have special places of natural beauty and serenity that preserve the original face of our land. They have been dedicated by Parliament for the benefit, education, and enjoyment of the people of Canada for all time. Each of the national parks contains unique, classic examples of distinctive scenery, flora, and fauna that are the natural heritage of all Canadians.

Enjoy the fresh air and take as many pictures as you like, but please leave the flowers and rocks for others to see after you are gone. The best souvenirs you can take home with you are the memories of your visit to one of Canada's national parks.

WHAT YOU CAN DO IN THE NATIONAL PARKS

Learn more about the natural history of our national parks in the world's most beautiful classroom—the great Canadian outdoors.

Try swimming at the fine beaches in Prince Edward Island, Gros Morne, Forillon, and Pacific Rim national parks, or treat yourself to a dip in the mineral hot springs at Banff, Jasper, and Kootenay national parks.

Trail-ride on horseback through the mountains in Banff, Jasper, Waterton Lakes, Yoho, Prince Albert, and Riding Mountain national parks or explore the wilderness areas of La Mauricie and Kejimkujik by canoe.

You will find excellent fishing at Terra Nova, Fundy, Cape Breton Highlands, and La Mauricie in the summer and ice fishing at Prince Albert and Riding Mountain in the winter.

The towering snow-capped peaks of Glacier, Kluana, and Auyuittuq national parks invite the experienced mountain climber, while the snowy slopes in Banff, Jasper, and Riding Mountain offer thrilling skiing for both beginners and experts.

You can practice your game of golf or tennis at Fundy, Jasper, Banff, Waterton Lakes, and Riding Mountain national parks. Boating is popular in many national parks and in some you can rent canoes and rowboats. Every park offers special enjoyment for the hiker, photographer, and nature lover.

Every park has a year-round interpretive programme to introduce you to the park and its special features. Have you ever wondered what causes avalanches, why bugs bite, or how to spot an animal trail? Talk to a park naturalist. Campfire talks, hikes, slide shows, and specially marked trails are some of the ways to discover more about our national parks. A schedule of interpretive events is posted on park bulletin boards.

Many national parks have facilities for handicapped visitors. These include extended-top tables, level camping areas and trails, washrooms, and special interpretive programmes. Ask for more information about these facilities from the park office.

PARK USER GUIDELINES

The national parks are open year-round. Most visitor services and facilities operate on a reduced scale from October to May.

PETS

Pets must be kept on a leash at all times in the park.

FISHING

You'll need a fishing permit to fish in park waters. The permit is valid in any national park. Permits can be bought at the information centre, administration office, campground, or warden's office in the park. A provincial or territorial fishing permit is required for fishing in waters outside most national park boundaries.

NO HUNTING

Hunting is not permitted in any national park, and possession of firearms is prohibited in many.

TOPOGRAPHIC MAPS

If you plan on hiking or backpacking off the beaten trail through the wilderness areas of one of the national parks, you will find a compass and a topographic map to be your best companions. Topographic maps show such important details as secondary roads, hills, valleys, creeks, and rivers.

ARRIVE PREPARED

Visitors to Canada's national parks should arrive equipped to fully enjoy the natural landscapes and recreational opportunities. The following list includes some of the items you may wish to bring.

Generally, bring what is reasonable to pack and transport to avoid disappointment if you cannot purchase or rent extra requirements locally.

Year-round:
- Camping equipment
- Hotel/Motel reservations
- Any specialized medication you require
- First-aid kit
- Matches/waterproof container
- Flashlight/lantern
- Backpack
- Binoculars
- Camera equipment/film

- Appropriate footwear for your intended recreational activity (wet-suit boots for diving; hiking boots; comfortable walking shoes; rubber boots; snowboots)

Summer/Spring/Autumn:
- Insect repellant
- Sunglasses
- Rainwear
- Warm clothing for cool evenings and surprise storms
- Hiking: topographic map, compass
- Fishing equipment

Winter:
- Layered clothing is the key to dressing appropriately for all temperatures. Start with warm underwear. Don't neglect head, ears, face, hands, or feet.
- Skiing: goggles, protective skin lotion
- Snowmobiling: spare parts/tools, helmet

BEARS

In the land of the great bear, man does not have the right-of-way.

When you travel from the city to the wilderness, you enter a different world with different rules.

You must be very careful not to attract bears by feeding them or leaving garbage where they can get at it. Illegal feeding of animals and careless garbage disposal create nuisance animals, which often must be destroyed to ensure the safety of park visitors. Garbage should be placed in approved containers only.

When entering a national park, talk to the park warden and his staff before going into the backcountry. They will give you sound advice and full help in making your visit a safe and rewarding one.

Published by authority of the Minister of the Environment, Canada.

Answers: 1. _____
_____
_____
_____

2. _____
_____
_____
_____

EXERCISE 25

This exercise will allow you to see how fast you can serve your purpose. Really push yourself to complete your purpose for reading.

Our Question: **1.** What evidence is there that prehistoric Woodland Indians may have practiced cannibalism?

Your Speculation: _____

_____

Our Question: **2.** What evidence might make you question their use of that practice?

Your Speculation: _____

_____

Delaware's Inhabitants of A.D. 900

A burial ground near Bowers Beach has become the most important link so far to the Indians who lived in Delaware long ago.

by Arthur G. Volkman

When Frank A. Webb and Sons, Inc., acquired a 200-acre farm near South Bowers Beach in Kent County in 1952, little did the Webb family suspect that the forefathers of the Delaware Indians slept in an unrecorded cemetery on the southeastern corner of the property bordering the Murderkill River.

Nor did anyone suspect the existence of the graves until the scientific curiosity of Ronald A. Thomas, Delaware state archaeologist, unearthed an important page of Delaware's history.

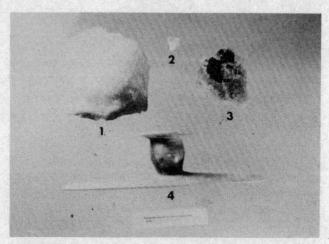

Among artifacts uncovered at the Indian Field Site, one is a human skull cap (1) cut into a dish, perhaps for ceremonial purposes. Also found were shark's teeth (2) used for pendants or arrowpoints, a mica sheet (3) and a platform smoking pipe (4). PHOTO BY ROBERT J. BENNETT

Today, the ancient burial ground, now called the Island Field Site, is believed to be the most important archaeological discovery ever made in Delaware. Its importance rests on these findings:

1) The presence of the largest number of skeletons—70 so far—ever to be unearthed in Delaware. The previous record was 52 skeletons found at the Townsend Site near Lewes along the Lewes-Rehoboth Canal.

2) The presence of a wide variety of intrusive artifacts, that is, tools and useful articles originating outside of Delaware, in this case, from as far away as the Finger Lakes region of New York State.

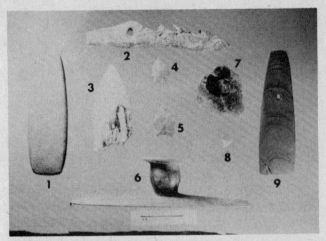

Useful objects buried with the dead included (1) adze blade of ground stone, (2) antler harpoon, (3) knife blade of Newark (Ohio) Chert, (4) "Jack's Reef Corner-notched" arrow point, (6) platform smoking pipe, (7) mica sheet, (8) shark's tooth and (9) pendant of Ohio banded slate. PHOTO BY ROBERT J. BENNETT

3) The presence of artifacts never before found in Delaware including a large smoking pipe, a dish carved from a human skull, harpoons and two conch shells of Delaware origin carved into drinking cups.

How did this cache of rich archaeological treasure come to life after more than 1,000 years of darkness?

Since Thomas' appointment as state archaeologist in January, 1965, he has been charting and investigating aboriginal sites in Delaware. In the course of this work, he has prepared a confidential map showing some 300 sites where stone

arrowheads, scrapers, axes, celts and other prehistoric Indian artifacts have been found.

Reports of Indian artifacts having been picked
up on the cultivated fields of the Webb farm led
the archaeologist to the site. In none of his previous investigations did he encounter a burial ground,
possibly because Delaware's damp and acidic soil
is not conducive to the preservation of skeletal
remains. But on the Webb property, for reasons
still to be explained, a peculiar soil composition
was apparently responsible for the preservation of
the human remains. (Amateur archaeologists working earlier have uncovered skeletal remains. See
Delaware's Buried Past by C. A. Weslager, University of Pennsylvania Press.)

Thomas rented a portion of the Webb property
in 1966 so that his work would not be interrupted.
His initial excavation that year produced a number of stone artifacts, a pottery vessel and one
grave in which the skeleton was found buried in
an extended position.

Encouraged, he returned in 1967 to pursue the
investigation, assisted by a group of college ma-
jors in archaeology employed for the summer
work by the state.

Imagine Thomas' astonishment when the 1967
excavations unearthed an Indian burial ground
that thus far has yielded 70 skeletons of adults
and children of both sexes. In addition, an un-
precedented number of 300 identifiable relics and
artifacts have been found in association with the
bones, evidently deposited for the departeds' use
in the after-life.

State Archaeologist Ronald Thomas carefully brushes earth from skeleton of female. Bones of an infant were found in her chest cavity, indicating double burial of mother, child.

Frank O'Shauntessy of the Archaeological Society of Delaware charts location of skeletal remains. Rope at top left and bottom criss-crosses site, marking off numbered rectangles for identification. Note teeth clearly visible at lower right.

Who were these people? No one is sure, but
Thomas theorizes that because of the large num-
ber of intrusive artifacts they were not Nanticoke
Indians, who inhabited most of the Lower Delmarva

Archaeologists found graves at more than one level. Two flexed
skeletons lie in repose close to soil surface, while several feet below
is the skull of another.

Peninsula when the first Europeans arrived in the 17th century.

Since tribal names probably originated with Europeans, prehistoric Indians cannot be identified tribally. Archaeologists prefer to apply the term "Woodland" to the prehistoric phase of Indian existence. The terms Late Woodland and Early Woodland refer to time sequences. The Indian graves at the Island Field Site have been tentatively identified as Middle Woodland, which dates from A.D. 700 to A.D. 1000.

The skeletons were arranged in several different ways, each of which yields important information concerning the burial practices of the tribe.

Several skeletons were disarticulated: that is, the bones were separated from the vertebrae or from each other. It was a practice on the Delmarva Peninsula for Indians to separate the joints of the deceased, to scrape the flesh away, and to let both dry before interment. Thomas thinks that this may have been done, or the bones may have been left with the flesh on in the air to dry until the flesh decayed.

Only two feet away from the disarticulated skeletons, archaeologists discovered three skulls, buried vertically one on top of the other, with one slightly to the side. These skulls apparently belonged to the disarticulated bodies buried nearby.

A large number of whole skeletons were discovered, many in flexed positions, that is, with the knees drawn up to the chest.

For the first time in Delaware, evidence was found of cremation. Scorched earth and bones indicated that one body had been burned *in situ,* or at the site, while two others had been burned elsewhere and the bones deposited with those of the *in situ* cremation.

The style of burial is related to the status of the deceased, says Thomas. More artifacts are found with non-cremated remains, seeming to indicate the decedent's ownership of more possessions.

Utensils were buried with the dead—as in Egyptian and Etruscan cultures—for their use in the after-life, and indicate that the Indians had a well-developed sense of religion and a firm belief in life after death.

The most important artifact uncovered was a large smoking pipe, the first of its kind discovered in Delaware. It was found near the body of a 10-year-old child, and while it did not belong to the child, it is believed that it was owned by a revered family leader and was buried with him or a member of his family. The Indians smoked tobacco, which they grew in the area, for smoking in pipes as part of a religious ceremony or for simple pleasure.

Another important find was a skull cap—a dish cut from a human skull. Not an item of everyday use, the skull cap was probably used in ceremonies. Never before found in Delaware, the skull cap leads the archaeologists to question whether these Indians practiced cannibalism.

Two conch shells carved into cups for drinking were found. These originated in Delaware. Thomas speculates that these may have been widely traded with Indians from other regions, in return for objects that were "imported," such as the large smoking pipe, harpoons for fishing and hunting, and cylindrical flakers—instruments fashioned from segments of deer antlers and used to cut and shape arrowheads.

Only one pottery fragment was found at the site. From this Thomas deduces that the site was primarily a graveyard for the main village, which was located elsewhere. Excavations of village sites generally turn up pottery fragments discarded or buried in pits with refuse.

If the Island Field Site was not used as a conventional burial ground over a period of time, then what precipitated a mass burial? Or were they slain by enemies? And how did the more shallowly buried skeletons escape mutilation by the plows of Delaware farmers?

The answers to these questions and others will be sought as work resumes on the excavation in warmer weather. The site is protected from the weather by a frame building, erected with funds contributed by an interested philanthropist.

While many questions remain, Thomas is convinced that these were not Nanticoke Indians. Rather, the intrusive artifacts point to a closer connection to Indians residing on Seneca Lake in central New York. The articles are identical to many excavated at the important Kips Island site there.

Furthermore, Delaware's site is the most distant from the Kips Island site to yield so many similar articles. Four or five such artifacts have been located on the Virginia mainland.

Thomas will write a report when the excavations have been completed, describing in detail each grave and its contents.

The state's first professional archaeologist, Thomas has done archaeological fieldwork in central Pennsylvania and in Arkansas. He is a graduate of Pennsylvania State University and the University of Arkansas, and is a former Teaching Fellow at the University of Pittsburgh.

He has added immeasurably to our knowledge of Delaware Indians before the arrival of the white man.

In his many reconnaissances of Indian sites, Thomas has been frequently accompanied by members of the Archaeological Society of Delaware, the Kent County Archaeological Society and the Sussex Society of Archaeology and History. The members of these groups, amateur archaeologists who have been combing the Delaware soil for many years, have acquainted Thomas with the locations of known sites and turned over data they have compiled. These persons prove invaluable to Thomas as volunteer laborers, for the state provides few funds for assistants to work with trowel and brush.

The pursuit of archaeology was not practiced in Delaware until the early days of the 20th century. It was not until 1953 that the General Assembly established the Delaware Archaeological Board, and it was not until 1965 that a professionally trained archaeologist was employed.

Public interest in the Island Field Site has been avid. The bones have not been removed from the graves, but have been carefully exposed by trowel and camel's hair brush, appearing in positions undisturbed since burial.

Used with permission of *Delaware Today* magazine, Wilmington, Delaware, Vol. 6, No. 6.

Answers: **1.** _____
_____
_____

2. _____
_____
_____

EXERCISE 26

When articles or stories we read are translated from other languages, there may be variations in spelling, sentence structure, and word use. Since you now know that your *purpose* questions focus your attention on potential answers, you should no longer be distracted by these inconsistencies with what you're accustomed to reading.

Our Question: **1.** What dangers threaten the future of orang-utans? How can their future be guaranteed?

Your Speculation: _____

_____

_____

Our Question: **2.** Based on this article and your past experience and knowledge, would you enjoy taking over Ulrike von Mengden's job? Why or why not?

Your Speculation: _____

_____

_____

Ibu Monjet, the German Mother of the Men of the Jungle

Ulrike von Mengden has a horse and a cat but most members of her family have tufted red hair and are lively and full of practical jokes—orang-utans. Forty-two of them.

For seventeen years she has not only been on the staff of the West German embassy in Djakarta but she also serves the national sanctuaries of Indonesia.

The Indonesians have difficulty grasping her complicated German name, so she is called "Ibu Monjet" (Mother of the Apes).

She is organised to look after the anthropoid apes. They are directly behind the livingroom of her house which is right in the middle of the zoo.

It is Sunday morning and the first rays of the sun indicate a hot day. A domestic cat lies sleeping on a portable cage. Through the mesh an ill baby orang-utan looks out with curiosity at what goes on in the yard beyond.

Anthropoid apes are dying out. They currently fetch up to DM30,000. Not much has been done about the species that is in danger of disappearing, but here they are not only out of cages but also out of the house.

One tries to get into a plastic bucket, which he has filled with water. Another envies him his amusing toy—and a fight quickly develops over the play thing. Others play about between the branches of the trees and the climbing poles. They take a bath in the sand or nestle up against "their mother."

Ragutan, that extends over 2,200 hectares, is the second largest zoo in the world, and for many years has been a refuge and shelter for threatened anthropoid apes, of which there are only a few still living.

In Malay orang-utan means "man of the jungle." They are friendly creatures that only exist in the virgin forests of Sumatra and Borneo.

In Sumatra coalmining and agriculture have taken up more and more of their natural habitat.

Last year in Borneo there was a forest fire that destroyed 3.6 million hectares of tropical rainforest.

When Ulrike von Mengden took over looking after the apes, hunters were the animals' greatest enemy. During the day the apes wandered about feeding off plants, in the evening returning to their nests in the tree tops.

The first danger to the animals was that it was believed their bones revived potency. Then private individuals wanted to have the apes for pets and if in capturing the young this meant killing the mother they were not particularly bothered about that. The threat has diminished in the meantime. "Earlier I had many more animals that would have been smuggled out," Ulrike von Mengden said, "but now we have a good environmental protection minister. Everything is being done to protect the species from dying out." When knowledge comes to light of an animal it eventually ends up in her zoo. There is not all that good a chance of saving animals, infected by human maladies which never attacked them when they were in the forest, even though at Ragutan there is a whole series of tricks to help the animals that have never appeared in any textbook.

Ulrike von Mengden had no experience of apes when she first came in contact with them in 1956.

It all began when the von Mengdens came to Djakarta in 1952. The Republic of Indonesia, made up of 13,000 islands, had only been a sovereign state for four years then. The West German embassy needed people that knew something about the customs of the country and, more importantly, knew something of the 250 languages spoken in the land.

It was not long before the von Mengdens got to know the director of the zoo.

In 1956 when the crowded zoo in the city centre was moved to the city suburbs the director asked Ulrike von Mengden if she could take over the anthropoid apes. She agreed immediately. As an incentive they were allowed to build a house in the middle of the zoo, and they live there to this day.

At the beginning there were many problems in dealing with the apes. There was, for instance, Felix. "His mother did not take to him." Ulrike von Mengden tried to bring him through, however. Feeding only meant that Felix did not die. He remained small and under-weight.

Ulrike von Mengden then spoke to the local people. From them she learned that the mother orang-utan chewed the food for her young when in distress. She learned a lot from the people in the district, for instance, that the Javanese used certain fruits to bring down a fever. She used them, successfully, with the animals.

Her love of the apes caused considerable amazement as well as the shaking of heads.

She tells of one experience. ''An officer came one day with an animal that was very sick. I fetched the vet, packed the ape in ice and then lay down with him in my bed and forgot the officer. He sat there and waited. Eventually he came to the bedroom and saw that the ape was lying in my bed.'' She admitted that many regarded her as mad.

In the virgin forest, orang-utans build their nests thirty metres up in the trees. There is no fence round their shelter but plenty of trees which is an open invitation to explore the area, but, said Ulrike von Mengden, ''It is amazing. They could disappear without any difficulty, but none of the animals go off.''

She attributed this to the fact that she does not allow strangers to come near the animals.

None of the apes in her zoo will ever be going back to the forest. She maintains that present conditions make that impossible, and she is sceptical about a re-habilitation centre in Sumatra.

The animals there are regularly plagued by spectators, which makes it impossible for them to live a normal life. They are more and more ''humanised.''

She believes that there would be better results from a similar project in Borneo. But she is waiting until there is enough free space given for the animals in which they can develop undisturbed by human beings.

Her own freedom of action is getting limited all the time and she is gradually getting used to the idea that one day she will have to say goodbye to her new home.

Her two children returned to Europe some time ago and she will have to return home when she is withdrawn from the West Germany embassy in Indonesia.

Behind the calmness there is a trace of sadness. Asked what is her greatest wish, she replied: "Naturally I would like to stay here, so that my work bears fruit."

Lars Wynter
(*Hannoversche Allgemeine Zeitung,*
27 October 1984).
Reprinted in *The German Tribune* No. 1157
(November 1984).

Answers: **1.** _____
_____
_____

2. _____
_____
_____

EXERCISE 27

One kind of **study-type** reading helps us to understand the attitude of the writer toward the subject. As a critical reader, you can then judge if the facts presented produce evidence that persuades you to agree with the writer or just shows his prejudgments. This type of reading is practiced with editorials and opinion articles. Use it with the following article.

Our Question: **1.** What is the writer's attitude toward his subject?

Your Speculation: _____

_____

_____

Our Question: **2.** Does the information he presents in the article persuade you to agree with him? Why or why not?

Your Speculation: _____

_____

_____

A Word About Words

by Mark Patinkin
Special to the *Courier-Post*

Bathroom plungers are no longer being called bathroom plungers. The new phrase, devised by a company that makes them, is hydroforce blast cup.

The Strand movie theater in Madison, Wis., has changed the name of its candy counter. It's now the Patron Assistance Center.

Maryland welfare applicants no longer meet with clerks. This year, they're meeting with eligibility technicians.

Finally, Campbell's has announced plans to put its soup in a new kind of container. The reason is cans are hard to open. The official explanation was a bit less direct. "The can," says Campbell's, "isn't as user-friendly as it used to be."

It has not been a good year for the American language. Boycotts became selective buying campaigns, bill collectors became credit analysts, tour guides became destination advisers and cemeteries began advertising pre-need arrangements.

On the theory that abuse can best be fought by exposing it, herewith, a 1984 rundown of felonies against English. Predictably, government has made the most interesting contributions.

The Canada Revenue Department apparently felt the word "quota" was too lowbrow. Now they call them "materiality of adjustments in relation to assigned workloads."

Word fiddlers on this side of the border, meanwhile, managed to improve on the phrase "revenue enhancement," that famous 1983 term for a tax hike. This year, they're calling them tax base erosion control.

One of the great examples comes from Congress. In an early Star Wars bill, the author managed to avoid referring to nuclear bombs in space. He called the bill the "People Protection Act."

The U.S. Justice Department felt it should not refer to the theft of the Carter briefing book as a theft. In its report, it called it the "transfer" of the book.

Moving to the varsity examples, we come, of course, to the military. Instead of calling for the overthrow of the Nicaraguan government, Undersecretary of Defense, Fred Ickles, urged its "unconsolidation." And we did not withdraw troops from Lebanon. According to the Pentagon, we "backloaded our augmentation personnel."

Another favorite comes from the State Department. In a human rights report, it found a new term for killing: "unlawful or arbitrary deprivation of life." The Food and Drug Administration earned second place in this category when it found "serious adverse effects" in the use of E-Ferol Aqueous Solution. The adverse effects were 38 deaths.

There's a third-place winner, too. The Trenton State Prison has a new name for its death row—the capital sentences unit. "It's not as bad as we thought, Honey. They're only sending me to the capital sentences unit."

It should be noted here that the District of Columbia Court of Appeals, in a ruling on lethal injection, says the drug being used must be certified ''safe and effective.''

Even educators, the presumed protectors of language, gave us a few. Bryant High School in Arkansas, wary of hurting students' feelings, no longer flunks them. These days, dumb kids get non-passing grades. In Amarillo, Texas, the school board has come up with an updated way of saying swim-time. It's now Aquatic Therapy.

Why all this felony English? Often, it's used as a coverup. A spokesman for Rolls-Royce in England recently insisted his cars do not break down. ''Occasionally,'' he explained, ''they fail to proceed.''

Instead of admitting his friends were on drugs, a college student was quoted as saying they had a ''pharmaceutical preference.''

A Rolls-Royce never breaks down. Occasionally, though, it "fails to proceed."

The Creedmoor Psychiatric Center in New York came up with a new way of saying a patient had been beaten to death. The patient, says Creedmoor, died of inappropriate physical abuse. Not to be confused with appropriate physical abuse.

Then there was a high form of art from Gen. Bernard Rogers, Allied Supreme Commander in Europe. He called civilian casualties collateral damage. "Hello. Sorry to bother you at home, but we'd like to report that a truck accident caused some collateral damage to your husband."

We should, perhaps, close by applauding those who tell it straight. Even if unintentionally.

A handout from the Wilson Center, a think tank, says its goal is to bring together historians, philosophers, scientists, and "people from real life."

Reprinted with permission from *Scripps-Howard News Service.*

Answers: **1.** _____
        _____
        _____

        2. _____
        _____
        _____

EXERCISE 28

Our Question: **1.** Based on your past knowledge and the information in this article, would you speculate that this presents an accurate picture of women in Australia? Explain.

Your Speculation: _____

_____

_____

Our Question: **2.** How do you think the rights of women in Australia compare with those of women in the United States?

Your Speculation: _____

_____

_____

Our Question: **3.** Are changes of the rights of women in Australia the results of the same influences as the changes of those rights in the United States?

Your Speculation: _____

_____

_____

Women in Australia

Women are a force for change in Australian society. The pride of place given to men as almost the sole shapers of Australian history is being challenged.

Today husbands more often than not share household chores, and more men are finding women alongside them in the workplace. It may be some time before there is a woman prime minister of Australia, but the need for women at the top—and their right to be there—is now widely recognised.

The growing role of women in the Australian work force is both a cause and a consequence of changing attitudes and lifestyles in Australian society.

In offices, laboratories and factories, in social and political organisations, women are making their presence felt. There are few remaining legal barriers against women in Australia in jobs, commercial contracts, politics and social life. The barriers that exist mainly stem from traditional attitudes built into society and not easily changed by new laws.

Women have brought about the most significant change in the Australian work force simply by entering it in thousands, and by seeking jobs which before were assumed to be suitable for men only. There are now women in Australia who drive buses, trams, taxis, racing cars and 50-tonne trucks. They are racehorse jockeys. They are apprentice electricians and mechanics. They are air-traffic controllers. They shear sheep and work as labourers. They are judges and Members of Parliament.

From the beginnings of European settlement in 1788—as a British penal colony—Australia was a male-dominated society. Men far outnumbered women. Only 15 per cent of the 150,000 convicts transported from Britain in those early years were women, and it was not until the 1850s that men and women began to be equal in numbers.

Australian history was seen as the history of men. Women, when noticed at all, were seen as playing confined roles in a shadowy background. A pioneering society considered that men did the real work of clearing and building, planting crops and raising herds, and moving goods and people across great empty distances.

One of Australia's best-known women poets, Dame Mary Gilmore, in her *Ode to Pioneer Women*, described them as "helpmates of men." They kept the home, raised the children and were expected to help their men in other ways. They played an important role—but a secondary one. The harsh conditions of pioneering in the vast continent and the social structures of the times seemed to reinforce this role, and women accepted it without much, if any, question.

Writing at the turn of the century about a group of women stranded without money in an isolated settlement, Henry Lawson, Australia's first great short-story writer, has one of his characters describe their predicament and conclude that "the fact that they is women is agenst [sic] 'em most of all." Feminists and others claim that this is still true of Australian women in general today.

In 1973 the Australian Government set up the Royal Commission on Human Relationships to

conduct a searching inquiry into the individual
and society. The commission made the status of
women an important part of its investigations. In
its final report, released more than three years
later, the commission found that women were
discriminated against in most areas. Discrimination was conscious, unconscious, and even built
into the social structure.

The report said: "It seems to us that history has
left us with a concept of male predominance, of
mateship and the image of the rugged Australian
male. This has little to do with the lives of most
Australians today. The problem now is how to
reconcile woman's traditional and domestic role
with her wider role outside the family."

The roles and relationships of men and women
have changed significantly. "Most of the measur-
able changes affect women but also have important effects on men," the report said. "As women
become capable of economic independence, men's
role as breadwinners for their families may seem
less significant."

The report said that "perhaps the most important change" was that most women in Australia
were able to control the number of children they
have. "As a result of smaller families and longer
lifespans, many are free of the responsibility for
caring for young children for the greater part of
their adult life," it said.

Some changes have been dramatic, others gradual. Taken together, they are altering the way
people live. They are challenging attitudes and
beliefs about women in the work force, male and

female roles in the home, community responsibility for child care, and family and personal relationships.

Carrying forward the momentum gained in the 1960s, women have seen a series of positive gains in the 1970s which no one seriously believes can be reversed. According to the historian and university lecturer, Dr. Beverley Kingston: "There is no way women in Australia will return to the kitchen and babies. It is hard to envisage what society and the position of women will be in the future—it will not be like anything we have seen before."

In Australia's population of 14,248,600 in June 1978, there were about 29,700 more males than females. Of slightly more than 7,100,000 females, about 5,170,000 were aged 16 years or more, and of these about half were in the work force—compared with about a quarter 25 years ago. Women now make up slightly more than one-third of Australia's work force.

Though virtually all occupations are legally open to women, most women are still concentrated in eight traditional female occupations: clerical, sales, typing, stenography, domestic service, process working, teaching and nursing.

The re-entry of older married women into the work force after their family responsibilities have lessened has gained momentum in recent years. It is now widely accepted that young women—like men—should be free to combine marriage with a career extending throughout their adult lives. The Australian and State Governments are paying spe-

cial attention to the handicaps women face in
competing for careers with men when the career
structure is based on the concept of a man working full time without interruption for his entire
career. Marriage barriers to job advancement for
women are now mostly gone. Maternity leave,
child-care facilities and job retraining provisions
are being extended.

Until about 10 years ago wages for women
were generally lower than for men. The federal
basic wage award for males was fixed taking into
account the needs of a man with a wife and
children to support. Female awards were generally fixed as a percentage of this. In 1969 the
Conciliation and Arbitration Commission—Australia's wage-fixing body—gave unlimited acceptance to the principles of equal pay for equal
work, and in December 1972 the commission
handed down a decision accepting unconditionally
these principles.

However, women in practice still receive less
on average than men. In October 1978 the average full-time weekly wage was $213 for men and
$169 for women. Among the reasons given for
the difference are the tendency for women to
receive less overtime work and fewer over-award
payments than men, and the concentration of
women in low-wage occupations. Equal pay provisions have been given as a major reason for the
massive increase in the number of women in the
Australian labour force.

Maternity leave was first introduced in Australia in the federal public service. It provides for 12

weeks on full pay, and—if the mother wishes—up to 52 weeks leave may be granted.

In March 1979, a Full Bench of the Australian Conciliation and Arbitration Commission decided to grant up to 12 months unpaid maternity leave to all women in the labour force following a national test case brought by the Australian Council of Trade Unions (ACTU).

More Australian men and women are married now than ever before. Fifty years ago only half the population over 15 was married; today the proportion is two-thirds. Three out of four Australians marry at least once, and most marriages produce children. Families of one and two children are the most common now—half the number in the first decades of this century.

As more married women get jobs, and as women seek careers with promotion opportunities, attention has focused on the provision of child-care facilities.

Government subsidies paid to child-care services reflect recognition by Australians of the need for such services, including day-care centres, family day care, pre-school kindergartens, play groups, private minding and work-based care. Australian Government spending on childhood services totals $69,000,000 a year.

The Australian Government has played an active role in dealing with the problems of women as employees and as citizens. It has financially supported many projects which have contributed to changes now taking place. On the advice of the Australian National Advisory Committee for International Women's Year in 1975, the Government made grants totalling more than $1,000,000 for projects on women's affairs.

In April 1978 the Government announced the establishment of a 12-member National Women's Advisory Council. The Council will give women a consultative voice at government level. Its main role will be to advise the Minister for Home Affairs on matters of concern to women in all walks of life, in the home, the work force and in the community generally. The Office of Women's Affairs also provides secretariat services for the National Women's Advisory Council.

Women in Australia did not have to struggle as they did in some other countries to break the male monopoly of the right to vote. Women in the Colony of South Australia were given the vote and right to sit in Parliament in 1894. Within a year of the federation of the Australian Colonies to form the Commonwealth of Australia in 1901, the national Parliament extended the federal vote to all women. The rights to vote in State elections and sit in State parliaments were progressively introduced.

The policymaking biennial congress of the ACTU adopted a charter on the rights of working women. It is regarded by the organisation as a necessary step to fulfil its policy of "the right to paid work for all who want to work irrespective of age, marital status, sex, sexuality, race, country of origin, political belief, or appearance." The Working Women's Charter covers education and job training, child care, health protection, equal pay and sex discrimination.

Fewer than 30 women were among more than 700 delegates at the congress which accepted the charter. Mrs. Jan Marsh, one of two ACTU research officers then, but now industrial advocate, said acceptance of the charter by an almost all-male congress showed that there was greater awareness than before of the needs of women in trade unions. The president of the ACTU, Mr. Robert Hawke, said: "I think we've made a bigger step forward in the period between the two biennial congresses than in the 50 years beforehand."

Union delegates met in March 1978 to consider ways of putting the charter into effect. The decision to bring on a test case on maternity leave provisions was among the first initiatives.

As women are now accepted in the work force, so is the feminist movement accepted as part of Australian society. Feminist and women's groups collectively have hundreds of thousands of members. They range from the long-established County Women's Association (about 80,000 members) which aims mainly at improving the welfare of country women and children, to small groups who may press for particular reforms or perhaps administer women's refuges and rape centres in the cities. There are, for example, women's groups who seek change by forming a co-operative to list or produce non-sexist books and encourage schools to use them so that children will grow up free of sexual stereotypes of the past. Others seek change through political lobbying. There are women's groups in teaching, the media, the public services, trade unions, consumer affairs, abortion law reform and the special problems of Aboriginal women.

Much basic research is being done to clarify the role and condition of women past and present, leading to a spate of reports, books, pamphlets and newsletters. For example, 18 researchers with an Australian Government grant spent a year compiling detailed listings of historical material about Australian women, now published as a series of guides. Reviewing them in a weekly newspaper, *The National Times*, Anne Summers—herself author of an analytical history of women in Australia—said the guides would lead to the change of at least some of the male-dominated stereotypes of Australian history.

In the same review, Anne Summers commented on the women's movement in Australia today: "The women's movement itself is now divided into at least two distinguishable groups: the respectable ones whose aims are largely accepted by government, even if they are somewhat slow to implement them; and the more radical, whose less tangible goals are expressed by the street demonstration or by a myriad of small press publications. It is the latter which still carry the radical impulse which characterised the early days of the new wave of feminism."

In an address to the Australia–Japan Relations Symposium in Canberra, Justice Roma Mitchell, who is now Chief Justice of the Supreme Court of South Australia, recalled that when she was an undergraduate in the 1930s many Australians—

both women and men—firmly believed that
"women's place is in the home."

"As a result, in most middle-class families a
secondary education was considered essential for
a boy but a waste of time for a girl," Justice
Mitchell continued. "At most the daughter of the
family might spend two or three years in secondary school." When the girl left school "she was
expected to be content with learning a few domestic skills before marriage."

Contrasting the role of Australian women today
with their role in the 1930s, Justice Mitchell
recalled that there were then few social service
benefits and no child endowment, and minimum
wages were fixed on the assumption that a man
had a wife and family to support but a working
woman supported only herself. The social climate
in those depression years, Justice Mitchell said,
was inclement towards those married women who
worked outside the home.

Last year, of about 160,000 university students
in Australia, 63,000—40 percent—were women.
The report of the Royal Commission of Human
Relationships said that women at university level
were more heavily concentrated in the humanities
and behavioral sciences and under-represented in
other fields. But changes were taking place, and
the proportion of women in medical schools had
been increasing steadily.

There is widespread awareness of factors in the
legacy of the past which today stand in the way of
girls and women making full use of the opportunities open to them in the Australian education

systems. This awareness is being translated into action. The Royal Commission on Human Relationships report said the necessary strategies for the role of education in improving women's status had been planned. "The will to change and acceptance of the need to change are essential to achieve educational equality for women," it said.

Education is compulsory for Australian children, and most schools are co-educational. Women in Australia have the same rights to post-secondary and tertiary education as men, and girls in increasing numbers are qualifying for entry to universities and colleges. The Australian Government has initiated a number of studies and other projects designed to encourage women to further their education.

Moves in recent years have been made by official, professional and special-interest groups to modify traditional attitudes about the status of women. Among these is the national Curriculum Development Centre's production of new learning material for social education, the attention which has been given to removing sexism from textbooks, and the introduction of women's studies courses in tertiary institutions.

The role of education in shaping the future society by imparting not only job skills and training but social attitudes and behaviour is well recognised. In commenting on this, the Royal Commission on Human Relationships gave an indication of the kind of society it would like to see developed in Australia.

"In our view," the report said, "[education] programs should emphasise the common humanity of males and females and develop the ability of men and women to co-operate and to share each other's roles and responsibilities in the family and in society without losing individual identity or the ability to develop the special potential of either sex."

Published for the Australian Information Service, Department of Administrative Services, by the Australian Government Publishing Service, Canberra.

Answers: **1.** _____
_____
_____

2. _____
_____
_____

3. _____
_____
_____

Surveying

Preface

Having reached this point in the program, you should be noticing a change in the way you go about learning. Learning should be growing easier for you—not just in this program, but in all subject areas that require reading. You should begin to realize that you are learning more in less time and remembering it better. You are becoming more efficient.

You have learned how important it is to set a definite purpose for your reading by asking yourself, "*Why* am I reading this?" After deciding on your purposes for reading, you have learned *when* and *how* to **skim**, **scan**, or **study** read. You've learned to predict or **speculate** on your answers, to bring all of your knowledge to the task to improve your comprehension and retention. You are now ready to use all these skills with one last tool for efficient reading: **Surveying.**

Surveying and **purpose setting** go hand in hand. **Surveying** materials often helps you set your purpose or makes your purpose more definite and clear to you. On the other hand, when you are assigned reading and your purpose is already set for you, **surveying** the materials available gives you an overview of the kind of information offered and determines the best approach to it. When the purpose is defined but resources are not assigned, **surveying** helps you select books or articles that will be most helpful in accomplishing your purpose.

The sequence in which you use the skills is designed to make learning as easy as possible. In actual practice, **surveying** is the first or second skill you use—depending on whether you are determining the purpose and resource materials or they are being assigned to you.

When you *know your purpose* for reading, you first **survey** to find the location of your answers. When you *are provided reading material*, you first set your **purposes**, the questions you want answered.

A flow chart might look like this:

1. **Purpose setting** or **surveying**
2. **Surveying** or **purpose setting**
3. **Speculating**
4. **Skimming—scanning—studying**, depending on purpose

With mastery of **surveying**, all the skills will fall into place, and you will have a process that will become habitual with practice.

Introduction to Survey Reading

When you meet a stranger and have a chance to chat with him or her, you learn something—usually enough to decide whether you want to continue the relationship. You also have a general idea of how to pursue this association if you want to do so.

When you buy property, you pay a surveyor to obtain clear boundaries of the lot. You want a map of what's included.

Surveying a book or an article that you are seeing for the first time gives you somewhat the same advantages. After **surveying** or prereading it, you have a general idea of the character, difficulty, and content. You also know the probable scope of information—the extent of the detail, the wordiness of the writing, the ease in finding your answers.

Learning to be a good **survey** reader will be helpful to you in two ways:

1. Deciding upon specific purpose questions
2. Discarding material not pertinent.

It will organize your thinking for your reading-learning attack to accomplish your purpose efficiently. It puts *you* in control.

Let's examine how to **survey** and do some exercises to become skillful. There is a definite sequence; the Ten Commandments of Survey are guides for that procedure.

The Ten Commandments of Survey

1. **Read the title, subtitle, and jacket summary** (if it is a book), **and identify the source** (author, committee, government, country, etc.).

   a. Have you heard about this piece of writing?
   b. Have you heard of this author? Read anything by him or her? Liked/considered him or her a believable source?
   c. Do you know anything about the subject in question before reading?

2. **Read the date of publication or copyright(s).**

   a. How current is this article or book?
   b. Does the date affect the worth of the material? Has more recent material made this outdated?

3. If there is an index, **analyze the index.** Your analysis will be a great timesaver in locating answers to questions connected with your purpose. Indexes are usually organized by one or more of these categories of contents:

   Subjects—places, dates, events, organizations, etc.
   Concepts—freedom, democracy, marketing, etc.
   Names—proper names, titles

   a. Which categories are emphasized: Subjects? Concepts? Names? Evenly divided?
   b. Which listings receive the most attention, have the greatest number of page references?
   c. What does the index tell you about the organization of the book and the focus of the author?

4. **Read any preface, foreword, and introduction.** Do any of them provide:

   a. The author's purpose in writing the book?
   b. The theme of the book?

5. **Read the table of contents. Note sequence, chapter summaries, reviews.**

   a. Note how the book is organized, the sequence and flow of ideas, the extent of material included.
   b. Check for chapter summaries, conclusions, reviews, and other study aids.
   c. Close the book and mentally review its organization and its value in accomplishing your purpose.

6. Flip through the book or article and **examine maps, graphs, illustrations, charts, bold headings, and study questions.**

7. **Read the first two or three paragraphs of the book and the last two or three.**

   a. Do you get the impression the material will be too basic, too difficult, too specialized for you and your purpose?
   b. Can you understand it?

8. **Read any summary or review.**

9. **Review your survey results and decide to use or not to use.**

    a. Does it appear that this material will satisfy your purpose?

    b. Will it provide the best and most complete material available, or would using another resource be more efficient?

10. **Finalize your purposes for reading** in the form of questions.

    a. Remember that our objective in **surveying** is to raise questions, not find answers.

    b. In forming your questions, use the six Question Words that can later guide you in selecting the most efficient method of reading to find the answers: *What, Where, When, Who, How, Why.*

At right is a summary of the **Ten Commandments of Survey.** After you complete the back of the page, cut it out to carry with you for reference until the process becomes automatic. You can use it at home, at work or school, wherever you read.

TEN COMMANDMENTS OF SURVEY

1. Read title, subtitle, jacket summaries, identify source (author, place).

2. Read the date of publication or copyright.

3. Analyze index — check emphasis of listings and their organization.

4. Read Preface, Foreword, Introduction.

5. Read Table of Contents. Note sequence. Check for chapter summaries.

6. Read maps, graphs, illustrations, charts, bold headings, study questions.

7. Read first two and last two paragraphs.

8. Read summary or review of book.

9. Review your survey results, decide to use or not to use.

10. Finalize your purposes for reading with WHAT, WHERE, WHEN, WHO, HOW, WHY questions.

EXERCISE 29

For our first practice in **survey**, let's return to an article you've already examined. **Surveying** it will demonstrate how this skill can speed the reading process. Turn back to page 110, the articles entitled **Canada** and **National Parks of Canada.** Since they were used as one source of information for Exercise 24, we'll treat them as one resource.

Obviously, some of the Commandments that apply to books (contents, index, preface) won't apply to articles, but let's use the applicable ones.

1. Read the title and identify the source. Speculate on the following questions:

   a. Have your heard of this source? _____

   b. Do you know anything about the source? _____

   c. Do you know anything about the subject? _____
   What? _____

   d. What would you expect to gain by reading this?
   _____

2. If there is a date of publication, what is it? _____
   Will this influence your acceptance of the material?
   _____

3. Read the index. What did you learn? _____

4. Read the preface, foreword, or introduction. What did you learn? _____

5. Read the table of contents. What did you learn? _____
   _____

6. Read maps, graphs, illustrations, charts, and bold headings. What did you learn? _____
_____
_____

7. Read the first and last paragraphs of the book. Will the material be difficult to read, pertinent to your needs?____
_____

8. Read any summary or review. What did you learn?____
_____

9. Review your **survey** results. Will the article be useful in answering your questions?
_____
_____

10. Finalize your purposes for reading. _____
_____
_____

Now let's look at the assistance the **survey** gave you.

1. The two titles, **Canada** and **National Parks of Canada**, are undoubtedly familiar to you. The sources are both departments of the Canadian government. Your reaction to government publications might be influenced by your past experience, but you probably accept these articles as factually correct.

2. 1984. You should undoubtedly check on specific regulations that pertain to you. Since you know the governmental divisions that had these articles printed, you

could contact them for the most recent information—or verify it with your travel agent. General information provided in these articles could still be helpful in planning your vacation.

3, 4, and **5** are not provided.

6. The map provides general orientation to Canadian provinces as well as the location of specific national parks.

The bold headings provide a map of the organization of the articles. The major division headings include:

Entry into Canada
Bringing Goods into Canada
Retention of Boats and Motors in Canada
Transporting Goods Through Canada
Seasonal Residents
Bringing Animals, Plants and Food into Canada
Taking Plants out of Canada
National Parks of Canada
What You Can Do in the National Parks
Park User Guidelines
Bears

Those headings enable you to find specific answers to questions. The subtitles (*From the U.S., From other Countries*, etc.) indicate even more specific areas to read—and the sections that don't pertain to your purpose for reading. The greatest timesavers tell you either what *to* read or what *not to* read to achieve your present purpose. At another time, you might have different purposes for reading and may need to read different sections of the same article.

7. Reading a small portion would probably reassure you that the information provided was factual and direct. The portion on national parks provides more opinion-type adjectives, but the objective is still to provide useful information.

8. There's no summary.

9. If you have not been assigned questions, you now know enough about the articles to be able to make your decision about using them to plan your trip.

10. Again, if you were reading these articles for personal use, you could establish specific questions you'd need to answer before your trip.

EXERCISE 30

This time select a book to **survey.** Choose one you plan to read—or at least would be interested in reading—but have not yet begun. Try to use a book with as many of the **survey** features as you can—table of contents, index, preface or foreword, illustrations, and bold headings. Your objective is to learn as much as you can as quickly as possible without actually reading.

1. Read the title and subtitle and identify the source. Speculate on the following questions:
   a. Have you ever heard about this book?_____
   b. Do you know anything about the author or source?
      _____
   c. Do you know anything about the subject?_____
      What? _____
   d. Is it necessary for you to read it? _____
      Why? _____
   e. What do you expect to gain from it? _____
      _____

2. Read the date of publication or copyright.
   a. How current is this material? _____
   b. Will it be worth your reading? _____
   c. Does more recent material outdate what the book offers? _____

3. Read the index entries.
   a. Are they organized by subject, concept, name, or a combination? _____

b. Which listings have the greatest number of references? _____
_____
_____
_____

c. What does the index tell you about the organization and overall content of the book? _____
_____

d. Will the apparent emphasis aid you in satisfying your purpose? _____
_____

4. Read the preface, foreword, and introduction.
   a. What is the author's reason for writing the book?
   _____
   b. Can you learn the theme of the book? _____
   _____

5. Read the table of contents, noting how many pages are contained in each of the major parts and subdivisions.
   a. Do subjects have about equal space? If not, which comprise major portions of the book? _____
   _____
   _____
   b. Are there chapter summaries, review questions, or other study aids? _____
   _____

6. Flip through the book looking for maps, illustrations, graphs, charts, and bold headlines. What is provided?
_____
_____

7. Read the first and last few paragraphs of the book. Do you get the impression that this book will be easy to read and understand? _____

8. If there is a book summary, read it and note key ideas.
_____
_____
_____

9. Review what you've learned from your **survey.** Will this book be of interest to you? Will reading it be of any special value? _____
_____

Which areas sound most interesting/helpful? _____
_____
_____

10. Finalize your preparation for efficient reading by developing specific purpose-setting questions using the Question Words:
    a. _____
    b. _____
    c. _____
    d. _____
    e. _____
    f. _____

Now you are prepared to read most efficiently and remember what you read.

EXERCISE 31

If it helps you feel more confident, keep the **Ten Commandments** at your side while you **survey** a longer article to which you may bring some previous knowledge.

This time, however, the questions are at the end of the article. So, **survey** the article, "Water-Supply Sources," as quickly as possible, and then answer the questions at the end. The objective that should guide your reading: to learn as much as you can about this article before you actually read it.

Water-Supply Sources
for the
Farmstead and Rural Home

Water-supply systems for farmsteads and rural homes may be developed from either ground water or surface water sources. Ground water sources are wells and springs. Surface water sources include streams, lakes, ponds, and cisterns.

A properly located and constructed well is the preferred source of water for domestic use. Well water is less likely to be contaminated than water from other sources. It is, however, apt to contain more dissolved minerals such as iron and manganese.

Surface water sources should be used only as a last resort because of the cost and difficulty of making the water safe to drink. However, surface water may be suitable for irrigating, firefighting, livestock, and other nondomestic purposes.

WATER REQUIREMENTS

QUALITY

Water for domestic use should be safe and pleasant to use.

Water may be unsafe because of its bacterial or toxic-chemical content. Contaminated water often carries disease-producing organisms or parasites. Surface water is almost always contaminated; well and spring water can become contaminated. Contaminated water can generally be made safe to drink by proper treatment.

Water may be unpleasant or unsatisfactory for use because of its chemical or physical quality. For example, excessive amounts of calcium and magnesium salts in water make it "hard." Hard water is less desirable for bathing, cooking, and laundering than soft water.

Suspended silt in water makes it look muddy or cloudy. Excessive amounts of dissolved minerals, gases, or decaying organic matter may give it a bad taste and odor.

CAUTION

A water's appearance and taste can be misleading. Many illnesses and deaths have resulted from drinking clean-looking, pleasant-tasting water from an unsafe source.

SPECIFIC INFORMATION

The occurrence of water and other conditions can vary widely from one place to another. Also, regulations and standards for developing a water-supply system may differ from one jurisdiction to the next. For these reasons, you will need to supplement the information in this bulletin with specific information about your particular area.

Local authorities are the best source of specific information. Talk with health officers, your county agricultural agent, Soil Conservation Service people, well drillers, and others. Here summarized are points to check on and questions to ask. Some are discussed in the text.

- What are the possible sources of a water supply? Which might be the best and perhaps the most economical?
- What are the laws regarding surface and subsurface water rights? They may vary in the different states.
- What quality requirements must be met in order to provide a safe and economical water supply?
- What tests of the water are required or recommended? Who makes these tests? Who evaluates the results?

Have your water tested for bacterial content and approved before using it. Tests for chemical and physical quality may also be desirable in many areas. Your local health officer can tell you what tests are necessary or recommended and

where you can have them done. He can also
evaluate the results.

*Never use water for domestic purposes unless it
has been approved.*

Your water may test unsafe or otherwise unsatisfactory. Effective economical treatment is not
always possible. You may have to consider alternative water sources.

QUANTITY

How much water will you and your family
need? How much will you need for your farm?
This table can help you determine your daily
water requirements:

Needed by	Gallons per day
Each	30–70
Each milk cow..	*35
Each horse, dry cow, or beef animal............	6–12
100 chickens	3–7
100 turkeys	7–18
Each hog	2–4
Each sheep...	2

*Includes both drinking water and sanitation requirements.

Lawn and garden watering are often important
water uses. For 1 inch of water on 1,000 square
feet of lawn or garden, about 700 gallons of water
are required. This amount allows for some loss by
evaporation or other causes.

Your water source should produce at least your minimum daily water requirements. If the source is a low-yielding well or spring, you may need a storage tank or cistern to supply water during periods of peak use.

GROUND WATER SOURCE

"Ground water" may be defined as the water in the ground that will move or drain freely by gravity.

It is the water in the zone of saturation—the zone beneath the surface of the ground in which all voids or openings in the rock and soil are filled with water.

The upper limit of the zone of saturation is called the water table or ground-water level. The water table is not flat—it follows the general contour of the earth's surface. It is higher under hills than beneath valleys. It may be near the surface or many feet below it. It may rise during rainy spells and drop during dry periods.

Water is sometimes confined above the main zone of saturation by impervious strata. It is then called perched water, and its upper limit is called a perched water table.

Ground water moves slowly but constantly toward points of lower elevation and may surface in springs, lakes, streams, rivers, or the oceans. It is replenished by precipitation (rain, snow, sleet, or hail) or irrigation that percolates down through the earth.

The stratum in the earth where the water occurs is called an aquifer. Wells are sunk down into an aquifer. An aquifer may cover hundreds of square miles. Water may travel a long way before it reaches your well or spring.

An aquifer may be "sandwiched between two impervious strata." The ground water is then likely to be under pressure in some places. It will rise in a well sunk through the dense upper stratum into the aquifer. This would be an artesian well.

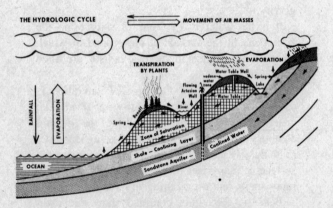

THE HYDROLOGIC CYCLE   MOVEMENT OF AIR MASSES

THE GROUND-WATER SYSTEM

The hydrologic cycle illustrates how water occurs in nature. Water within the zone of saturation is ground water—the source of water for wells and springs.

HYDROLOGIC CYCLE

There is a continuous exchange or circulation of water between the earth and the atmosphere. This is called the hydrologic cycle.

Water evaporates into the atmosphere from the oceans, and the winds carry the moisture-laden air over the land. Water also evaporates from the ground, from vegetation, and from lakes, rivers, and other bodies of water.

The water falls as precipitation—rain, snow, sleet, and hail. Part runs over the surface of the ground and returns via streams and rivers to the oceans. Part is utilized by the vegetation and returned to the atmosphere by transpiration. Part percolates down through the porous formations of the earth, becomes ground water, and eventually reaches the sea.

Ground water is the source of water for wells and springs—the recommended sources of water for rural domestic use.

WELLS

Proper location and construction of a well are extremely important. Numerous outbreaks of waterborne diseases have been directly attributed to faulty well construction that permitted the entrance of contaminated water.

Wells may be dug, bored, drilled, driven, or jetted. All but drilled wells are limited to loose, unconsolidated formations containing few large rocks.

Considerations in choosing the type of well include: Ground formation, desired yield, depth of the water table, characteristics of the aquifer, and construction costs.

Drilled wells are usually constructed by well-drilling contractors because of the special equipment and skill required. Many jurisdictions require that all types of wells be constructed by licensed well drillers. Even where not required, construction by a well driller is recommended. Good workmanship and proven experience are important in well construction.

Don't choose a well driller on the basis of price alone. One driller may quote a higher price than another, but he may also provide a better well. For example, he may drill deeper for better-quality water. Or, he may do a better job of sealing the well against contamination. Or, he may use a better grade of casing. A safe, adequate water supply is most important.

If you have a particular well driller in mind, check his work with your local health officer or with neighbors for whom he has recently constructed a well. For mutual protection, some sort of written agreement with the well driller is recommended. It should cover general construction specifications, cost, and payment arrangements.

CAUTION

There is no known safe distance at which a water well may be located from an uncased waste-disposal well.

Disposal of waste into the ground water should never be permitted unless extreme precautions are taken to prevent the contamination of wells. The cost of the required investigations and construction to insure noncontamination makes it impractical to use a waste-disposal well on farms with water wells.

LOCATION

Locate a well above and as far as reasonably possible from known or possible sources of contamination. Minimum recommended distances are:

Source of contamination	Minimum distance (feet)
Waste disposal lagoons	300
Cesspools	150
Livestock and poultry yards	100
Privies, manure piles	100
Silo pits, seepage pits	150
Milkhouse drain outlets	100
Septic tanks and disposal fields	100
Gravity sewer or drain not pressure tight	50
Pressure-tight gravity sewer or drain	25

Wells should be located for ease of maintenance and service. No permanent structure that would interfere with servicing should be built over a well. When located adjacent to a building, the well should be at least 2 feet beyond the drip line of the eave. Overhead utility lines should not interfere with erection of the driller's boom.

Reprinted from *Farmer's Bulletin*, U.S. Department of Agriculture.

Questions

Now you are ready to record what you recall from your **survey.** Fill in all the information you can, then resurvey the article to fill in any areas left unanswered.

1. Title of the article: _____
2. Author: _____
3. Section or chapter title: _____
4. Have you ever heard about this article? _____
5. After reading the title, author, and italicized print, what do you think the article is about? _____
   _____

6. After reading the first two or three paragraphs and the last two or three paragraphs, I learned the following:

   Key idea: _____
   Key idea: _____
   Key idea: _____
   Key idea: _____

7. Judging from my **survey,** including the paragraphs I read, I would expect to find reading it to be (circle one):

   Difficult   Easy   Average

   I would probably use _____-type reading (fill blank).

   Skim   **Scan**   **Study**

You should now fully understand the reading technique of **survey.** The use of the **Ten Commandments** will become automatic with continued use. The benefits of surveying material before you read it should also be apparent. Many students find that learning to become a good surveyor is one of their most valuable learning skills. It saves time by eliminating unnecessary reading that doesn't serve their needs and enables them to learn more quickly and efficiently. It provides a basis for making the decision to read or not to read—an essential step in managing the time you spend reading.

E X E R C I S E   3 2

Before trying to **survey** books as the first step in learning from them, **survey** the following articles from *Aluminum Developments Digest*. Use any of the **Ten Commandments** that apply to aid you in developing an overview of what this periodical offers and how it might serve your needs or interests. **Do not read the articles; use only your survey skill.**

Review what you have learned from your **survey.**

_____

_____

_____

_____

_____

_____

_____

_____

_____

_____

Now that you have a clear overview of the information included and the organization of the articles, the next step is to use this new information to determine your purposes for reading the *Digest*. These *purpose* questions will guide your reading—both what to read and how to read it.

Write at least three *purpose* questions about what you would like to know about recent developments in aluminum. After each question, write your **speculation** of what you think the answer will be.

1. Your Question: _____
   _____
   Your Speculation: _____
   _____

2. Your Question: _____
   _____
   Your Speculation: _____
   _____

3. Your Question: _____
   _____
   Your Speculation: _____
   _____

Aluminum
Developments Digest

A Resource for Educators   Winter 1984-85

Angel Planas, chief
inspector at Turner
Industries, Irwindale,
Calif., checks the
propane flame of the
lightweight Olympic
torches.

ALUMINUM LIGHTENS OLYMPIC TORCHES

For the 8,700-mile relay from New York to the 1984 Summer Olympics in Los Angeles, officials asked for more than 4,000 torches combining light weight with maximum flame duration. So Turner Industries of Irwindale, CA, made them out of aluminum.

The flame bowl of each torch was formed of alloy 1100-0 by metal spinning. The handle, drawn tubing of alloy 6061-T6, formed the reservoir for liquid propane with a vapor pressure of about 150 pounds per square inch. Turner says the design was calculated to withstand 5,000psi and was tested to 1,100psi, the limit of the test equipment, without bursting.

The torch's external design is classically—but deceptively—simple. Inside is a complex system for safe fuel control: at the bottom, a combination fueling and safety valve; at the top, a modified "Schrader" (automobile tire) valve controlling propane flow; and just below that, a screw-in needle valve for bleeding or emptying the reservoir.

An "orifice block" six-thousandths of an inch in diameter limits the maximum propane flow from the Schrader valve to the burner tip in the bowl.

Chemically engraved with Olympic symbols, bronze plated, and with leather-clad handles, most torches carried a half-hour of fuel and weighed only 2 pounds 4 ounces.

SURVEY SAYS PROFESSORS LIKE ALUMINUM

A survey of 204 engineering professors, conducted for the Aluminum Association last May, shows that educators feel they need more information about aluminum, but what they already know they like.

Aluminum won high marks on environmental acceptability, recyclability, durability, strength-to-weight ratio, and its reputation as a high-quality product.

More than two-thirds of the professors expressed a favorable "overall opinion" of the aluminum industry.

More than 64 percent rated aluminum highest for recyclability. And 52 percent gave it highest grades for "having a quality image with consumers," far outranking plastic and steel.

When compared to steel and plastics, aluminum also drew more votes as the industry which "has paid the most attention to producing things environmentally acceptable," for "being durable, lasting the longest," and for having the best strength-to-weight ratio.

Despite the recognition of aluminum's qualities, educators said steel often gets the most attention in under-graduate classes, mainly because of its traditional use in architecture and civil engineering.

Architects, civil engineers, and mechanical engineers, in fact, led the survey respondents in expressing a desire for more technical information on aluminum.

More than 50 percent of the professors wanted more information, in particular, on the product forms of aluminum; almost 56 percent wanted more information about its properties and characteristics.

And more than 64 percent said they would welcome additional information on designing for aluminum.

The survey was sponsored by the Aluminum Association as part of a continuing program to assess and serve the needs of the academic community.

Dr. Kirit Bhansali (left), Dr. Joanne Murray and Dr. Archie McAlister review the equilibrium phase diagram for the aluminum-germanium series at the National Bureau of Standards in Gaithersburg, Md.

COMPUTERS EVALUATE ALUMINUM IN
PHASE DIAGRAM RESEARCH

At the National Bureau of Standards in Gaithersburg, MD, metallurgist Joanne Murray punches keys, and her face lights up along with the VAX computer screen.

"There," she says. "That's the sexiest thing we can show you."

Painting itself across the tube is a colorful three-dimensional prism, its upper-section carved into hills and valleys like a chunk out of the Maryland countryside.

But it's not a "landscape." It's the mathematical surface of a ternary alloy phase diagram, generated by powerful new software still under development.

And it's a milestone, measuring how far the Phase Diagram Data Program, conducted in conjunction with the American Society for Metals, has come in only a few years.

The program has completed and published critical evaluations of nearly 300 alloy equilibrium phase diagrams, most of them binary (two-metal) systems, and has developed numerical and graphic-display databases.

At least 29 aluminum binary system diagrams and nine aluminum ternaries have been evaluated so far. Murray and Archie McAlister, also of NBS, are the aluminum category editors.

"Ultimately, we expect to complete 2,800 binary system evaluations," covering almost all bi-metallic diagrams, Kirit Bhansali, leader of the NBS team, told ADD.

The evaluated data and computer programs can be used to analyze and extend binary diagrams, and even to generate diagrams of higher order alloys lacking experimental data.

"One aim is to improve the theoretical basis so we don't have to rely entirely on empirical data," Bhansali explained. "You need binaries to help build the higher order systems."

A phase diagram depicts the solid and liquid phases and the crystal structures that can coexist in alloys at various concentrations and temperatures. It's a basic tool of metallurgy.

The standard compilation, Max Hansen's *Constitution of Binary Alloys*, published in 1958, has been updated only to 1964. There is no single compilation of higher order alloys. And even existing data are often uncertain, Murray pointed out. The ASM/NBS program's expert evaluators reexamine the original experimental determinations and the resulting diagrams.

"It's surprising how much disparity there can be in what people see," Murray said. Alloy contamination can go undetected, equilibrium temperature measurements may be inaccurate, microstructures may be misinterpreted.

"It's only when you collect all the observations that you see the disparities," she added.

The need for critical review and updating was apparent, and in 1978, ASM and NBS agreed on a pilot program. It was expanded in 1981, and moved into high gear in 1982 as funding rolled in.

ASM handles fund-raising and the publication and dissemination of the project's output; ASM's

Metadex bibliographic database, maintained since 1966, is an important resource for the evaluators.

NBS performs some of the evaluations, receives others from evaluators throughout the world, and develops the computer programs.

ASM and NBS also coordinate international cooperation in the program.

About 30 experts now evaluate binary phase diagrams and another 20 work on the ternary (three-metal) systems.

William W. Scott, ASM technical director, reports that at least 58 companies and agencies have provided major funding. The Aluminum Association is a leading supporter of the program. ASM has raised about $4 million to set up the program, which is expected to become self-supporting through the sale of publications and a computer search service.

New evaluations appear in the Bulletin of Alloy Phase Diagrams, now published six times a year.

ALUMINUM SOLAR LOUVERS CONTROL BUILDING CLIMATE

The energy-saving, award-winning Occidental Chemical Building in Niagara Falls, NY, shows what serendipity can do.

Serendipity—the unexpected discovery—gave the building its distinctive sun-tracking aluminum louvers; and that success gave the louvers, designed for a quite different purpose, a brand new market in solar control.

The award-winning Occidental Chemical Building in Niagara Falls,
N.Y., is equipped with movable solar louvers that are governed by
a computer linked to solar sensors.

The louvers consist of rectangular frames spanned
by movable blades almost 15 feet long, governed
by a computer linked to solar sensors. More than
300 units, sandwiched between glass walls, regu-
late the passage of heat and light through all four
walls of the square building while affording spec-
tacular views over Niagara Falls, the river gorge
and the city.

Cannon Design, Inc., of Grand Island, NY, the
architect-engineer, estimated the building would
consume energy at a rate of only 33,000 Btu per
square foot per year, less than half the typical rate
in that climate.

Project manager Charles Arraiz says the building, fully occupied since February, 1983, is performing at least that well, and maybe better.

Cannon's engineers ''happened to run across''

the aluminum louvers during their design studies, he says.

The Moore Co. of Marceline, MO, had developed them in 1977 for airflow control as a companion-product to its large heat-exchanger fans. The louvers reflect that purpose.

Each blade is roll-formed of .032-inch alloy 5052-H291 sheet into a hollow airfoil shape 8 inches broad and 2 inches through at its thickest. The airfoil contains a corrugated stiffener of alloy 5052-H38, and is welded shut along its thin edge.

Control rods and bearing shafts are alloy 6061-T6, and frames are alloy 6063-T6.

Blades weigh just over a pound per square foot and show no visible deflection over horizontal spans up to 16 feet, a key esthetic factor in their choice for the Occidental building with its panoramic views.

Built to withstand corrosion, hailstones and the weight of snow and ice, the aluminum louvers have been installed outside in other solar applications, exposed to the weather.

They control sunlight through the glass atrium roof of The Solarium, a multistory building in Denver. And louver installations have been designed for Lehigh University in Bethlehem, PA, the Georgia Tech Bookstore in Atlanta, and dozens of other buildings from Portland, OR, to New Orleans, and from Flemington, NJ, to San Diego.

Peggy Kitchen, Moore's chief engineer, says the Occidental building was the first to demonstrate the versatility and value of the aluminum louvers in climate control; since then, sun-control has become their largest market.

WASHINGTON MONUMENT'S ALUMINUM
SHINES AFTER A FULL CENTURY

What is probably the first architectural use of aluminum in the United States, if not the world, has just completed a full century of service exposed to the weather, without maintenance.

It's the small pyramidal apex installed, on Dec. 6, 1884, atop the Washington Monument.

Aluminum was an inspired last-minute choice for that unique application. Lt. Col. Thomas Lincoln Casey, in charge of construction, had planned to install a copper lightning rod and decided to shape it into the tip of the monument itself. Only six weeks before its planned installation to complete construction, Casey wrote to a Philadelphia metallurgist, William Frishmuth, about plating this apex with platinum.

Frishmuth offered a better idea: make it of aluminum, and skip the plating. Aluminum, he noted, is a good electrical conductor and it would withstand the weather without staining the white stone below.

Frishmuth was then the only producer of aluminum (1,800 ounces in that year) in the United States and was patenting a process he claimed would drastically reduce its cost, which rivalled that of silver.

He kept an exasperated Casey waiting while he displayed the aluminum apex at Tiffany's jewelry store in New York, publicizing himself and his patent. He delivered it only a week before the planned capping ceremony—scarcely time enough to engrave the ceremonial inscriptions on it.

The apex was as pure as the contemporary production process could make it: 97.75% aluminum, 1.70% iron, and 0.55% silicon.

It weighed 100 ounces, and measured 5.6 inches square at its base and 8.9 inches tall.

From the ground 555 feet below, the closest most people could ever see it, the apex is barely visible; but that did not deter the irrepressible Frishmuth from advising Casey to wipe the small aluminum point after installing it, "so it don't show finger marks."

Priscilla McMaster, a student at the University of Cincinnati, won the Aluminum Association's food can logo contest with this design.

STUDENT TAKES TOP CAN LOGO PRIZE

A just-graduated design student from the University of Cincinnati has won the $5,000 first prize in the Aluminum Association's nationwide competition seeking graphic logos to identify recyclable aluminum cans.

"Happy would be an understatement. I'm ecstatic," said 24-year-old Priscilla McMaster of

Cleveland, Ohio, after learning that her design was selected from more than 2,000 entries.

The second-place prize of $2,500 was awarded to Gerald Gallo of Graphics by Gallo, Washington, D.C.

Third place and $1,500 went to Paul Matson of RAHM Advertising, Oakland, CA.

Kerry Polite of Polite Design, Philadelphia, PA, won the $1,000 fourth prize.

The contest for student and professional designers sought logos which: emphasize creatively the recyclability of aluminum; are appropriate for commercial application; may be printed on paper and foil labels or embossed directly on aluminum food cans; and are distinctive even in small sizes.

Announcing the contest last winter, Association President John C. Bard said, "About 5 percent of the food cans on the market today are aluminum. We see this market expanding as food companies and consumers come to realize the advantages of aluminum, especially its recyclability. Recycling aluminum saves about 95 percent of the energy needed to produce the metal from bauxite ore. With more and more aluminum food cans appearing on supermarket shelves, consumers will need a way to distinguish aluminum from other packaging materials."

McMaster's first-place design makes sophisticated use of the visual figureground phenomenon: its dark and light areas are seen, alternately, as a dark can against a light background, a light can on a dark ground, or a streamlined letter *A*, for aluminum. The shifting between positive and negative images suggests recycling and "reinforces the idea that aluminum takes form well," her entry said.

McMaster was still a senior student when she submitted her logo to the competition.

"It was the second one I did," she told ADD. "I had about five designs I thought had some potential, but I came back to that one because it had a kind of simplicity that seemed to work well."

McMaster said she and her classmates learned of the competition from an enthusiastic university instructor, Stan Brod. "One of the posters was sent to the university," she said. "He brought it to the class and encouraged us to enter."

ASSOCIATION FUNDS REDUCTION RESEARCH

The Aluminum Association has agreed to sponsor a new group at Carnegie-Mellon University in Pittsburgh, PA, to conduct fundamental research on aluminum reduction.

Paul J. Sides, assistant professor of chemical engineering, is to be the principal investigator; consultant Rudolph Keller is to serve as program manager and technical adviser.

The Association will provide $130,000 a year in support of the research under an initial three-year contract.

The proposal by Keller and Sides suggested augmenting research done by individual companies "by pooling resources to sponsor a research program at an academic institution," and said no such group exists in North America to focus on light metal production.

Sides told ADD in an interview that one of the first projects planned by the group is research on the interface between molten aluminum metal and the molten cryolite floating on top of it in an electrolytic reduction cell. The aluminum serves as cathode, while the electrolyte also contacts a carbon anode.

"Although the energy loss in cells is proportional to the distance between anode and cathode, there is a limit to reducing that gap, because the interface between the metal and the electrolyte is not flat, but wavy," Sides explained. "The gap must be large enough to prevent molten aluminum from contacting the anode and to allow carbon dioxide gas to escape. The topography of the molten pool is quite important for cell operation.

"Also, some people think there's a layer of electrolyte between the pool of aluminum and its cathode substrate, and that's bad news. It might get down there, against gravity, by a capillary flow mechanism. That also needs study."

Although the Hall-Héroult process has been used for nearly a century, the Carnegie-Mellon proposal pointed out that environmental and energy considerations have spurred improvement efforts.

"As the present production processes are refined and as new systems are considered for development," it said, "the benefits derivable from fundamental knowledge of the chemistry and physics of the processes become more and more evident."

BENEFITS OF ALUMINUM RAILCARS GROW CLEAR

In the reviving railroad freight car market one bright spot is the inroad made by cars built largely of aluminum.

Aluminum cars had entered the railroad market more than twenty years ago but were held back then by their cost. Now, economic conditions have changed.

"I think the penetration of aluminum into the railcar market is going to stay with us this time," says Gary J. Baker, vice president for sales and marketing of Pullman Standard Manufacturing Division of Trinity Industries.

Steep price increases on diesel oil in the 1970s have put a premium on fuel efficiency.

"The railroads, competing with the truckers in a deregulated environment, are looking at anything they can do to reduce their operating costs," Baker told ADD. "And one of the largest factors is the cost of diesel fuel."

Aluminum offers substantial weight reduction and easier forming into aerodynamically efficient designs, both significant fuel-savers. Building a car body of aluminum instead of steel can cut the empty weight of a 62,000-pound car by almost one-third—ten tons less for the locomotive to pull.

Also, aluminum resists the acid formed when the sulfur in coal comes into contact with water; many steel coal-cars must be rebuilt after about 15 years because of severe corrosion.

Of some 1.5 million operable railcars in the United States, about 10,000 are aluminum, Baker says.

The number of new cars built each year has collapsed from a 25-year average of 64,000 to only 6,000.

In the past year, however, about 1,000 of these new cars were aluminum, Baker says, "a pretty impressive percentage of the market, although it's a depressed market."

He expects the market to recover slowly—not all the way, but perhaps to 50,000 cars a year; and he thinks production of aluminum cars will increase with it.

"Probably two-thirds of the car builders have some form of an aluminum car, particularly a coal car," he said. "And it will continue. It will get into other car designs as the business starts to pick up."

Baker adds that lingering concerns among some railroad people about maintaining and repairing aluminum cars are being overcome.

"I think the Aluminum Association has done a tremendous job of explaining that aluminum need not be any more difficult to work with than steel cars," Baker volunteered. "I think it's starting to pay off."

VACUUM BRAZING MYSTERY LINGERS

In recent years, cost advantages of fuel-saving weight reductions have made aluminum a rapidly growing replacement for copper and brass in automobile radiators.

But that growth is spurred by a manufacturing

technique that relies, in turn, on a minor metallurgical mystery.

General Motors had used an all-aluminum radiator, brazed in molten salt, in its Corvette in the 1960s. In that process, all salt residues must be removed to avoid corrosion problems.

GM's Harrison Radiator Division told ADD the process was appropriate for the Corvette, but not for the high-volume production required for other GM models. The company engineered improvements in long-term corrosion resistance and in manufacturing costs before returning to aluminum radiators in 1980 on some of its Chevrolet and Pontiac station wagons.

At the same time, GM abandoned salt-brazing for vacuum brazing.

Ford began using aluminum radiators, assembled mechanically, in its 1982 Escort and Mercury Lynx; but Ford also switched to vacuum brazing in 1983.

Chrysler, now using aluminum radiators on its Omni, Horizon, Charger and Turismo subcompacts without air conditioning, has not announced further plans; but Ford and GM have been expanding their use of aluminum.

Ford plans to put aluminum radiators into 90 percent of its North American cars in 1988.

In vacuum brazing—the key to this expansion—aluminum heat-exchanger parts are assembled and heated in a vacuum to about 1100 degrees F. At that temperature, an aluminum-silicon cladding alloy fuses and joins the parts into an integral solid structure. After cooling, the radiator is completed by crimping on plastic tanks.

The enemy of aluminum brazing is the oxide film formed by exposure to air, which would block the bonding by fused aluminum.

Brazing in a vacuum prevents immediate reoxidation; but something must—and does—disrupt the oxide in the first place, and therein lies the mystery.

Clad aluminum alloys 3003 and 3005 are commonly used in radiator structures. Automotive and aluminum experts believe that magnesium, emerging in the high heat, plays a vital role in disrupting the oxide. But they're not sure.

There are different theories, they say: that magnesium directly reduces the oxide; that magnesium does not dissociate, but somehow breaks up the oxide film; or that thermal expansion breaks the oxide and magnesium only scavenges residual atmospheric oxygen, preventing reoxidation.

The question can be resolved, they say, only through further research.

RESISTANCE SPOT WELDING
PRESENTS RESEARCH CHALLENGE

The application of current resistance spot welding research to production operations is vital to increasing the use of aluminum in automobiles.

Despite recent breakthroughs which improve weld quality, consistency and the tip life of electrodes, there is also a need for further research on metal surface characteristics, process feedback control, and nondestructive quality control techniques, according to a report by the Aluminum Alloys Committee of the Welding Research Council.

"Perhaps the greatest research challenge in the joining of aluminum is to develop equipment and procedures that will provide assurance that high-quality, consistent joints will be made," says the report, prepared by Ed Patrick and James Dowd.

Patrick told ADD resistance spot welding is a key to use of sheet aluminum in auto bodies because "it's a relatively simple method, it's fast, and the auto industry would like to keep on using it."

Surface characteristics are important because contaminants or aluminum's oxide coating can increase electrical resistance and create hot spots that shorten the life of the copper welding electrodes. Research shows that a rough outer surface reduces resistance, extending electrode life, because the tight electrode clamping can disrupt the oxide film.

Development of a feedback system could improve weld quality. One approach might be to measure resistance across the parts with a relatively low electric current and allow that reading to control automatically the welding current, producing more uniform welds.

EUROPEANS REVISE GUIDELINES FOR ALUMINUM STRUCTURES

The western European structural metals industry is expanding and revising its design recommendations for aluminum structures.

Wallace W. Sanders, Jr., professor of civil engineering at Iowa State University, reports that the plans call for new design guidelines dealing with fatigue, friction grip connections, and the "Plastic hinge theory" of design.

The aluminum structure recommendations issued (despite its name) by the European Convention for Constructional Steelworks (ECCS) in 1978 are not directly used in the United States, but their revision could influence U.S. construction practices indirectly.

Their American counterparts are the design recommendations of the Aluminum Association, a major resource for public authorities in drafting building codes. The ECCS and the Aluminum Association watch developments in each other's recommendations with interest.

Sanders attended a recent meeting of the ECCS Aluminum Alloy Structures Committee in Liege, Belgium, with partial financial support from the Aluminum Association.

ECCS design recommendations for fatigue in aluminum construction are "still in the developmental stage," Sanders told ADD. "Tests of full-sized structural elements are under way now at the Technical University of Munich. The results will be used for the recommendations, which are expected in the latter part of next year."

Also being drafted is a section adding recommendations for "plastic design." Sanders said this approach emphasizes the load-carrying ability of a complete structure, as distinguished from the more conventional "elastic design" approach emphasizing element-by-element load limitation.

Another new section will cover friction-grip connections, in which bolts are tightened to a specified torque or additional bolts are used, to establish a non-slip connection between structural elements. Sanders said, "Friction grip connection has the potential for replacing welded construction in load-reversing applications."

ALUMINUM DEVELOPMENTS DIGEST

Published three times yearly by the Aluminum Association as a service to educators.

* * *

A. Stephens Hutchcraft, Chairman
John C. Bard, President

Thomas R. Pritchett, Ph.D.
Peter R. Bridenbaugh, Ph.D
Dennis D. Foley, Ph.D.
John A. S. Green, Ph.D.
Rodney E. Hanneman, Ph.D.
Norman A. Nielson
Rodney J. F. Thorpe
Paul V. Mara

THE ALUMINUM ASSOCIATION, INC.
818 Connecticut Ave., N.W.
Washington, D.C. 20006

_____

Answers: **1.** _____
            _____
            _____

            2. _____
            _____
            _____

            3. _____
            _____
            _____

Rapid Reading—Fiction

You've come a long way in this program:

    You have learned to **survey** the printed material offered by a writer to become familiar with the type and scope of information included.

    You know the value of establishing specific **questions** to guide your method of reading.

    You can take inventory of your previous knowledge and opinion of the subject by **speculating** on the answers to your questions before you read.

    You have been applying these skills to all your reading to increase your efficiency.

You are now ready to master the skill many people believe is the most difficult: **rapid reading.** It's difficult because it requires you to break old habits and form new ones. You did some changing when you let your **questions** determine your rate and method of reading, when you read to find answers rather than to look at each word on the page. Now you're going to work even harder to break the habit of reading word-by-word. For a while, we also ask that you not expect complete comprehension.

To practice **rapid reading**, you will need two paperback fiction books. Select two that you have not read. To make the practice of a difficult skill as easy as possible, choose books with few characters and a simple story line. This is not necessarily the time to tackle a difficult classic.

Learning new skills is not easy. Learning to tie your shoes took lots of practice; now you do it without thinking. The same was true of driving a car or typing or shaving. You must master the technique before you can expect speed.

In **rapid reading**, also called **pacing**, you're going to be asked to look at words so rapidly that you cannot possibly pronounce them or think of their meanings. After some practice, you will comprehend a few words; later you will begin to grasp thoughts. But the only way to begin is to force yourself to do the uncomfortable.

Think of your mind as a rubberband. Each time you read more rapidly than is now comfortable, you stretch your ability. When you release the tension—read at any speed you wish—you will find that your zone of comfort has expanded. As you practice, you will also find that your comprehension increases.

Moving Your Eyes Faster Than Your Mind

For over one hundred years, experts in the fields of medical and psychological research have concluded that most humans use only 4 percent to 10 percent of their mental abilities, of their potentials to learn, to think, to act.

That's one reason why you are using *Super Reading*. You want to reach your potential. You want the skills that will make you comfortable and competent with any learning task.

You've seen how using **purpose** questions and **speculating** reduces the time needed to learn when reading. Using questions to direct thinking and making a creative leap through predicting answers are two of the "get ready" skills, skills that prepare your mind to learn with greater efficiency.

Rapid reading or **pacing** is a skill for improving the efficiency of eye movement based on the mechanics of that movement. Although it may not be apparent at first, the result will be improved comprehension in less time. When wedded to the other *Super Reading* skills, **pacing** completes a system for efficient, effective reading. The complete system invites you to develop your potential ability to process the explosion of information generated in today's fast-paced world.

What's Wrong with the Old Way?

Fact: Most adults are still reading the way they were taught in elementary school. With the addition of more reading in school or in everyday exposure, their reading rate has probably settled around 250 words or so a minute. Yet the same adults can think at rates of 600 to 1,000 words a minute. A difference in these two rates creates an interesting problem. The mind is in high gear while the eyes are seeing in low. Thinking is much more rapid than seeing.

What happens when this difference occurs to you? You

lapse into boredom or daydreaming, your mind wanders to what you want to do over the weekend or what you'll have for dinner. You find yourself rereading the paragraphs you just finished. You find disconnected thoughts difficult to understand and remember. You have a problem, and the problem needs a solution.

Why do most adults have this problem? Let's review the reading instruction you received in elementary school. First, you learned the alphabet symbols and learned to put into words the sounds that those symbols represented. You read each word aloud. Then you progressed to reading phrases and sentences—aloud. In about the third grade you were expected to read silently and understand what you read— still word-by-word. You were pronounced "A Reader." "Subvocalization" was your method of pronouncing the words silently. Unfortunately, when you learn to read aloud, subvocalization is the natural result. This habit carries into adult life. Even if you no longer subvocalize, you may look at almost every word on the page.

As you climbed through the grades of formal education, you probably never had anyone teach you *not* to read word-by-word. You didn't learn to read groups of words or the ideas represented by the words—although you may have developed your own method to reduce the time you spent on required reading.

Another block to good comprehension when reading slowly is regression—reading the same words two or three times. As you reread, your ability to remember fades, and you begin doubting your ability to remember at all. You reread more, lose more trust in your memory, and finally conclude you don't understand what you're reading. Your motivation to read is also gone.

The Benefits

Accelerated reading can reduce fatigue and increase motivation. If you read 200 words a minute and have a 10,000-word report to study, it will take you one and a half hours to read it—word-by-word. Reading a report of that length for that long can be as fatiguing as digging a ditch. If you read at a slow rate, you probably dread lengthy reading tasks and put them off as long as possible. Reading slowly is a drain on your patience, concentration, and interest in learning.

You may be surprised to learn that faster reading usually improves comprehension. Your level of concentration is higher. Unfortunately, our early training seemed to indicate that to read slowly and carefully meant understanding and remembering more. That is not necessarily true. Keeping our minds engaged by what we are reading is much more important than slowly progressing down the page. When the difference between your reading rate and your thinking speed is too great, you have too much time to be distracted by things or people around you, by physical discomforts, by personal concerns.

Another benefit is the improvement of your completeness of thought. An analogy might be watching a three-hour movie, ten minutes at a time. It would be difficult to keep the plot and characters clearly in focus; it would be a memory test.

There is an optimun reading speed for maximum comprehension. This rate will vary from one task to another, and finding your most effective rate for the resource you are reading is critical for good comprehension. Like completing a jigsaw puzzle, the fewer and larger the pieces of information, the faster they form the picture you seek.

Rapid Reading

Let's look at two very different ways to read. One is the way you were taught to read in elementary school; the other is the way you will learn to read using the **pacing** skill.

Look at Example A. Each word has a dot over it. When you read word-by-word, your eyes stop to look at each word. In this example, your eyes would stop 197 times. If each stop took one second, it would take more than three minutes to read page 10 in *The Lilies of the Field*.

Example A

The Lilies of the Field

accepted, as he accepted the days that came to him. He lived his life one day at a time. There was laughter in him.

He was a buck sergeant when he received his Army discharge at Fort Lewis. The Army years had been good to him and he had accumulated a sum of money through some slight thrift, much moonlighting and occasional gambling luck. He bought a secondhand station wagon in Seattle, equipped it for sleeping, and started out to see the West. He had not believed much of what he heard in the Army and he did not believe the tales that Westerners told about their country; he was, however, a curious man.

On a morning in May, Homer Smith drove into a valley west of the Rocky Mountain Range. Spring, which had stood aloof from him on the higher levels, moved down the valley to meet him. Blue, yellow, and pink flowers twinkled in the tawny expanse of buffalo and grama grass. He had grown up in South Carolina, a far different land from this. On his left, as he drove south, blue- and purple-tinted mountains tipped with snow formed a

Look at Example B. The center half of the page is identified by two vertical lines separated by a shaded area. This center area is where your **pacing** technique will be used.

Example B

The Lilies of the Field

accepted, as he accepted the days that came to him. He lived his life one day at a time. There was laughter in him.

He was a buck sergeant when he received his Army discharge at Fort Lewis. The Army years had been good to him and he had accumulated a sum of money through some slight thrift, much moonlighting and occasional gambling luck. He bought a secondhand station wagon in Seattle, equipped it for sleeping, and started out to see the West. He had not believed much of what he heard in the Army and he did not believe the tales that Westerners told about their country; he was, however, a curious man.

On a morning in May, Homer Smith drove into a valley west of the Rocky Mountain Range. Spring, which had stood aloof from him on the higher levels, moved down the valley to meet him. Blue, yellow, and pink flowers twinkled in the tawny expanse of buffalo and grama grass. He had grown up in South Carolina, a far different land from this. On his left, as he drove south, blue- and purple-tinted mountains tipped with snow formed a

10

Dots are placed above the words in the **pacing** zone. By reading only the dotted words, you reduce your reading time by about half. But you don't reduce your comprehension by half. That's because you're thinking beyond the words your eyes are seeing. You're getting enough ideas from what you are reading to piece together generalities. Your mind is completely engaged by what you are reading.

Try reading only the dotted words in the **pacing** zone. Notice that you are still obtaining enough information to know that this is setting the scene for a story: the character and a bit about his background and personality, the location and time of year.

Let's go one step further in the process of thinking more and seeing less. You don't even have to focus on each word in the center half to get the information you need to understand.

Look at Example C. In reading the circled words, you select words in each line of print, first near the left vertical line and then near the right. You fix your eye on each word for a split second, sliding back and forth in a Z or S pattern to the bottom of the page. Try to stop on information words—nouns, verbs, adjectives, and adverbs.

Now you're down to 26 stops, and your eyes are sliding over another 100 or so words. All the time your eyes are seeing, your mind is putting together ideas. At first you may remember only 3 or 4 words from each reading. Your objective is to go past the literal act of remembering isolated words to mentally collecting and relating ideas. For some, this takes *a lot of practice*, so don't give up.

The first ten to fifty times you use this technique you can expect to be frustrated. But if you stay with it, practicing daily, you can develop more efficient patterns of eye movement. The most notable result will be better concentration when

Example C

accepted, as he accepted the days that came
to him. He lived his life one day at a time.
There was laughter in him.

He was a buck sergeant when he received his Army discharge at Fort Lewis.
The Army years had been good to him
and he had accumulated a sum on money
through some slight thrift much moonlighting and occasional gambling luck. He
bought a secondhand station wagon in
Seattle, equipped it for sleeping, and started
out to see the West. He had not believed
much of what he heard in the Army and
he did not believe the tales that Westerners
told about their country. He was, however,
a curious man.

On a morning in May, Homer Smith
drove into a valley west of the Rocky
Mountain Range. Spring which had stood
aloof from him on the higher levels, moved
down the valley to meet him. Blue, yellow, and pink flowers twinkled in the
tawny expanse of buffalo and grama grass.
He had grown up in South Carolina, a far
different land from this. On his left, as he
drove south, blue- and purple-tinted
mountains tipped with snow formed a

using any of the *Speed Learning* skills. And good concentration is critical to effective reading.

Eventually you can develop the use of this technique
further; instead of staying within the two vertical lines, you
can slide back and forth, selecting words that are most
informative. **Remember? your objective is to collect and
organize information as rapidly as possible.**

As you practice with Example D, try to stop on nouns, verbs, adjectives, and adverbs. Also notice that as you focus on a word, you are aware of other words around it—immediately before and after, above and below it. This peripheral vision is always present and can be very helpful. Your eye includes these extra words automatically and adds to your information. For example, the words you remember from the first few lines might be:

> accepted (his) life, laughter, (buck) sergeant, Army (discharge)

Those aren't complete thoughts, but you have enough information from reading 8 of the 38 words to develop a mental picture, to understand what the writer is giving you. You are also concentrating. Your mind doesn't have time to wander. And since you are constantly organizing the information you are receiving, you will remember it. By practicing the **pacing** technique until you are comfortable with it, you will be developing efficient reading. Begin practice with Example D.

Now let's get ready to **pace** a whole book. First we'll share a technique for preparing a paperback book for reading. Unlike hardcover books that are bound or stitched, paperbacks use glue to hold the pages in place. If you bend the pages back sharply to make the book lie flat, the glue breaks, and the pages fall out. If you don't make the book lie flat, you have trouble seeing the portion of the pages next to the spine, and the book closes when you put it down unless you turn it face down—and that breaks the glue. But there is a solution!

Example D   *The Lilies of the Field*

accepted as he accepted the days that came
to him. He lived his life one day at a time.
There was laughter in him.

He was a buck sergeant when he received his Army discharge at Fort Lewis.
The Army years had been good to him
and he had accumulated a sum of money
through some slight thrift, much moonlighting and occasional gambling luck. He
bought a secondhand station wagon in
Seattle, equipped it for sleeping, and started
out to see the West. He had not believed
much of what he heard in the Army and
he did not believe the tales that Westerners
told about their country; he was, however,
a curious man.

On a morning in May, Homer Smith
drove into a valley west of the Rocky
Mountain Range. Spring, which had stood
aloof from him on the higher levels, moved
down the valley to meet him. Blue, yellow, and pink flowers twinkled in the
tawny expanse of buffalo and grama grass.
He had grown up in South Carolina, a far
different land from this. On his left, as he
drove south, blue- and purple-tinted
mountains tipped with snow formed a

10

Preparing a Book for Pacing

It is important to loosen the book you are going to **pace**. This is to let the pages lie as flat as possible so it will be easier to turn them.

1. Place the book binding flat on your desk or table with the edges of the pages upright.
2. Pull the front cover down to the desktop and run your fingers firmly down the inside of the cover closest to the binding. Be firm in bending the pages without breaking the binding. This will result in the front cover staying open and not crowding the inside pages.
3. Repeat Step 2 with the back cover.
4. Repeat the same folding technique using the first several pages in the front of the book and then the first several pages in the back until you reach the center.

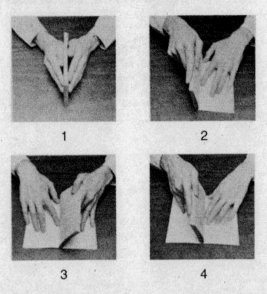

Survey Your Book

The first step in **pacing** is to **survey** your book using as many of the **Ten Commandments** as are appropriate. Few fiction books have indexes, prefaces, forewords, introductions, or summaries. Usually the publication date does not influence the use of the book for enjoyable reading.

On the other hand, most paperbacks have many teasing hints about the plots, settings, characters, and conflicts. If the author has written previous best-sellers, the publisher is certain to mention it. Many have maps and illustrations. Use anything provided to give you a framework for the story before you read it.

Notes from **Survey**:

_____
_____
_____
_____
_____
_____
_____

Separate the information you've learned into three categories:

People—who they are and what they do in the story.

Events—what the action is/will be.

Conflict—what ideas, activities, positions will be the focus of the plot. Conflicts are caused by the confrontation of two opposing forces. One force is usually a person or group of people who opposes other people, forces of nature or society, or someone else's control. Speculate what problems must be solved before the end of the book.

People: What they are/do:

_____   _____
_____   _____
_____   _____
_____   _____
_____   _____

Events:

_____
_____
_____
_____

Possible Conflicts:

_____
_____
_____

Speculate how you think the story will unfold—and end.

_____
_____
_____

Pacing Technique

1. Place the book flat in front of you. Using one hand as a pacer, move it smoothly down the page. If you find your moving hand distracting, use the smaller side of a 3 x 5-inch card. The reason for a pacer is to keep your eyes moving down—not across—the page in their habitual direction.

2. When you reach the bottom of the page, jot down any words you remember. If you don't remember any, don't let it upset you; you'll improve with practice. Try to focus on nouns, verbs, adjectives, and adverbs—information words. Later, after the technique is comfortable for you, you can connect the words into thoughts.

3. Practice this technique one page at a time until you feel comfortable. Then try two pages before writing. Keep adding until you can **pace** a complete chapter before catching your breath and reviewing what you've read.

4. Speculate what you think will happen in the next chapter.

Now you're ready to **pace** your first fiction book. Follow the steps carefully; you're changing long-used habits and attempting to establish now ones. Skipping steps in haste or impatience now will seriously limit your ability to use the skill later. During this learning period, each time you begin a new book:

1. **Prepare** the book for **pacing.**
2. **Survey** the book and **speculate** on the unfolding of the plot.
3. **Pace** a page and recall what you've read. Continue pacing, covering longer sections until you complete entire chapters before reviewing.
4. At the end of each chapter, write a brief summary of the chapter.
5. **Speculate** what's to come.

EXERCISE 33

Pace your first fiction book. You'll need a timer to indicate when to stop reading. If you prefer, have someone time you. You cannot think of keeping time as you learn to pace.

Begin by spending **15 seconds on a page**, stopping at the end of each page to jot down words or phrases you remember. Progress to **30 seconds for two pages.** By the time you are reading four or five pages before stopping, try to decrease your time to **10 seconds a page—1 minute for six pages.** Try to develop a steady pace and maintain it.

1. Prepare your book for pacing.
2. Survey the book. You have done this.
Chapter 1
3. Pace the first page in 15 seconds. Note what you remember.

_____

_____

Page 2 Recall

_____

_____

Page 3 Recall

_____

_____

Page 4 Recall

_____

_____

Page 5 Recall

_____

_____

Page 6 Recall

_____

_____

If you still feel unable to handle two pages, continue practicing with one page at a time for a few more pages. As soon as you can, push yourself to increase the number of pages read to two, then three, and so on. Stop at the end of the chapter.

Recall
_____
_____

Recall
_____
_____

Recall
_____
_____

Recall
_____
_____

Recall
_____
_____

Recall
_____
_____

4. Write a brief summary of the chapter—facts, events, and conflicts, not complete sentences.

_____
_____
_____
_____
_____

5. Speculate what you think will happen in the next chapter.

_____

_____

_____

_____

Continue using the same pattern for chapter 2, chapter 3, etc.

_____

_____

Chapter 2
Stop at the end of the chapter.
Recall

_____

Recall

_____

Recall

_____

Recall

_____

Recall

_____

Recall

_____

Write a brief summary of the chapter—facts, events, and conflicts, not complete sentences.

_____

_____

_____

_____

Speculate what you think will happen in the next chapter.

_____

_____

_____

Chapter 3
Stop at the end of the chapter.

Recall

_____

_____

Recall

_____

_____

Recall

_____

_____

Recall

_____

_____

Recall

_____

_____

Recall

_____

_____

Write a brief summary of the chapter—facts, events, and conflicts, not complete sentences.

_____
_____
_____
_____
_____

Speculate what you think will happen in the next chapter.

_____
_____
_____
_____

Chapter 4
Stop at the end of the chapter.
Recall

_____
_____

Recall

_____
_____

Recall

_____
_____

Recall

_____
_____

Recall

_____
_____

Recall

_____
_____

Write a brief summary of the chapter—facts, events, and conflicts, not complete sentences.

_____

_____

_____

_____

Speculate what you think will happen in the next chapter.

_____

_____

_____

Chapter 5
Stop at the end of the chapter.
Recall

_____

_____

Recall

_____

_____

Recall

_____

_____

Recall

_____

_____

Recall

_____

_____

Recall

_____

_____

Write a brief summary of the chapter—facts, events, and
conflicts, not complete sentences.

_____

_____

_____

_____

_____

Speculate what you think will happen in the next chapter.

_____

_____

_____

_____

Chapter 6
Stop at the end of the chapter.
   Recall

_____

_____

   Recall

_____

_____

   Recall

_____

_____

   Recall

_____

_____

   Recall

_____

_____

   Recall

_____

_____

Write a brief summary of the chapter—facts, events, and conflicts, not complete sentences.

_____
_____
_____
_____

Speculate what you think will happen in the next chapter.

_____
_____
_____
_____

Chapter 7
Stop at the end of the chapter.
Recall

_____
_____

Recall

_____
_____

Recall

_____
_____

Recall

_____
_____

Recall

_____
_____

Recall

_____
_____

Write a brief summary of the chapter—facts, events, and conflicts, not complete sentences.

_____
_____
_____
_____
_____

Speculate what you think will happen in the next chapter.

_____
_____
_____
_____

Chapter 8
Stop at the end of the chapter.
  Recall

_____
_____

  Recall

_____
_____

  Recall

_____
_____

  Recall

_____
_____

  Recall

_____
_____

  Recall

_____
_____

Write a brief summary of the chapter—facts, events, and
conflicts, not complete sentences.

_____

_____

_____

_____

_____

Speculate what you think will happen in the next chapter.

_____

_____

_____

_____

Chapter 9
Stop at the end of the chapter.
   Recall

_____

_____

   Recall

_____

_____

   Recall

_____

_____

   Recall

_____

_____

   Recall

_____

_____

   Recall

_____

_____

Write a brief summary of the chapter—facts, events, and conflicts, not complete sentences.

_____
_____
_____
_____
_____

Speculate what you think will happen in the next chapter.

_____
_____
_____
_____

Chapter 10
Stop at the end of the chapter.
Recall

_____
_____

Recall

_____
_____

Recall

_____
_____

Recall

_____
_____

Recall

_____
_____

Recall

_____
_____

Write a brief summary of the chapter—facts, events, and conflicts, not complete sentences.

_____
_____
_____
_____
_____

Speculate what you think will happen in the next chapter.

_____
_____
_____
_____

Chapter 11
Stop at the end of the chapter.
Recall

_____
_____

Recall

_____
_____

Recall

_____
_____

Recall

_____
_____

Recall

_____
_____

Recall

_____
_____

Write a brief summary of the chapter—facts, events, and conflicts, not complete sentences.

_____

_____

_____

_____

_____

Speculate what you think will happen in the next chapter.

_____

_____

_____

_____

If you have more chapters in your book, use extra paper.

The next step in enjoying a fiction book is to formulate questions you want answered now that you know the framework of the plot. Since you're familiar with the people, the sequence of events, and the conflicts, returning for more detail or to enjoy the beauty of descriptive passages is not a guessing game. You may find that you know all you really want from this book.

EXERCISE 34

Pace a second fiction book, following steps 1 through 5 as in Exercise 33. You'll find this second exercise much easier—and more comfortable. You probably won't have to begin by pacing one page at a time unless there has been a time lapse since you completed the first book. Progress at your own rate. Your goal should be to read several pages—possibly a chapter—before stopping to make notes of people, events, and conflicts you have read. It is advisable to stop at the end of each chapter to summarize and speculate. Eventually, with practice, you can eliminate that pause in your reading, but most people are not ready to read whole books without stopping after practicing with only one novel.

1. Prepare your book for pacing.
2. Survey the book. What did you learn?

   _____

   _____

   People

   _____

   _____

   Events

   _____

   _____

   Conflicts

   _____

   _____

3. **Pace** at 10 seconds a page, stopping at the end of each chapter or more frequently to jot down notes.
4. Write a brief summary of each chapter.

5. **Speculate** what you think will happen in the next chapter.

_____
_____
_____
_____
_____
_____
_____
_____
_____
_____
_____
_____
_____
_____
_____
_____
_____
_____
_____
_____
_____
_____
_____
_____
_____
_____
_____
_____
_____

Rapid Reading—Nonfiction

Having learned the fundamental principles of **pacing** or rapid reading with fiction, you are now ready to apply them to the more challenging reading of nonfiction.

Although you frequently gain some knowledge from reading fiction, your purpose is usually to be entertained. In the reading of nonfiction, your purpose is more specific and demanding. In many cases, reading a textbook, trade journal, report, or instructions from the State Motor Vehicle Department or IRS is not reading of your choice. You might consider it ''assigned'' reading. Your need for information necessitates your reading. Since the older we get, the more of this demand-type reading is required of us, we must learn a quicker, more efficient way of getting the job done.

Let's remember our goal: **efficient reading.** Sometimes speed is possible, sometimes it's not. Think for a minute about a lawyer's reading-learning tasks. They are like yours in many ways. Obviously, a lawyer is not going to use the pacing technique when analyzing a legal contract or a new law. However, all the skills (**survey**, **skim**, **scan**, **study**, and **pacing**) serve specific purposes in gaining background knowledge and an understanding of the organization of the material. Without a firm foundation and organization of thoughts, there is no basis for evaluation, interpretation, and application of new information.

You now have all these skills in your mental tool chest, and you will apply all of them at various times in nonfiction reading. Keep in mind that your *purpose* for reading nonfiction is critical. You must keep asking yourself, "Why am I reading this?" You must answer yourself by stating as specifically as you can, "I want to learn the *What*, *Who*, *When*, *Where*, *How*, and *Why* about this subject." Be precise. Your mind is going to have to sort through nonfiction information to find everything that pertains to your need, your purpose for reading. All other information must be ignored to let you comprehend clearly and retain what you need. Even when you find the extraneous information interesting, if it does not serve your present purpose, spending time with it detracts from your efficiency.

Let's examine the procedure for reading nonfiction. We'll work with nonfiction books. If your material is not in book form, use only the portions of the procedure that apply. This **learning pattern** applies to all nonfiction.

Learning Pattern for Nonfiction

1. Answer the following question as completely as possible. Your answer is your **purpose** for reading.

What do I want to learn from this material?

2. **Survey** the book or article using all of the Ten Commandments that apply.

3. Using the information from your **survey**, reexamine your answer to number 1. Clarify your **purposes**, being as specific as possible by using the Question Words as guides.

4. **Speculate** the answers to the questions using your past experience and knowledge and your **survey** as your base.

   Note: *Take the necessary time to do steps 1 through 4. It will take a small portion of your overall time, and can reduce your task dramatically. Spending this time increases both your efficiency and the effectiveness of your learning.*

5. **Read** to satisfy your **purposes.** Read flexibly, with your questions guiding you to use of the most appropriate skill: **skimming, scanning, studying.**

   A. Check yourself periodically to see that you have not relapsed into reading whole pages when they don't serve your purpose.
   B. Use your pencil to check margins for important ideas, answers to specific questions. If you must learn the material precisely for reference or examination, write your questions in the margin next to the answers. (If the book is not yours, take notes on 3 × 5-inch cards.)

6. If your overall **purpose** demands it, organize your thoughts in outline form.

A. State the most important ideas or concepts pertaining to your purpose—answers to the most important questions.

B. Under each idea stated, list related facts, people, dates, places, ideas, or quotations that serve your purpose. Be brief, using as few words as possible.

Learning Aid

Some students have difficulty moving from their **survey** information (step 2) to good *purpose* questions. Purpose questions accurately express your learning needs, your real intent for using a particular book or article.

If you have found visual aids helpful in seeing relationships, in directing and organizing your thinking, you may find the Question Ball useful. Try it to begin your thinking.

In the center of the Question Ball, write what you think is the main subject of your book.

In each question partition, write what you want to learn to achieve your purpose. Proceeding through this determination of questions gives you a quick inventory of what you know and what you want to learn. Your reading will be guided by the questions.

Sometimes, of course, there isn't an answer to each question, but the use of the Question Ball will provide you with a clearer overview of relationships, sequence of events, and unknowns that must be found in some other source.

To practice using the skills in nonfiction material, we suggest that you select three different kinds of material. Books are often most helpful, but if all your nonfiction reading is in company reports or professional journals or some other source, use three of them.

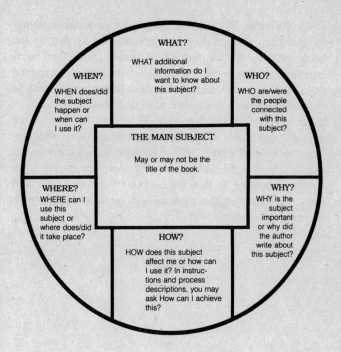

WHAT?

WHAT additional information do I want to know about this subject?

WHEN?

WHEN does/did the subject happen or when can I use it?

WHO?

WHO are/were the people connected with this subject?

THE MAIN SUBJECT

May or may not be the title of the book.

WHERE?

WHERE can I use this subject or where does/did it take place?

WHY?

WHY is the subject important or why did the author write about this subject?

HOW?

HOW does this subject affect me or how can I use it? In instructions and process descriptions, you may ask How can I achieve this?

For the first exercise, use **reference** material. It might be a cookbook or discussion of nutrition, an atlas, a travel guide, or an encyclopedia. For example, you may need to do research about the metric system. Find a book on the subject and complete **Exercise 35.** Develop questions that you can't answer, and apply your skills in finding answers. We don't usually want to learn all the facts in a reference book, so decide what portions of the book serve the purpose you have established and don't waste your time on the rest. In using a telephone directory—probably our most frequently used reference book—looking for John Smyth's number does not include reading all the other numbers in the book.

For **Exercise 36**, select a **biography** or **autobiography** for practice. Be certain to undersand *who* is writing the book and *why*. Are all parts of the person's life given equal attention? Are personal experiences of the person interpreted or judged by someone else? Are there portions you'd like to remember? Take notes as we have discussed.

Your selection for **Exercise 37** should be a resource dealing with some discussion of philosophy or religion. Your questions might help you find time sequences of events, cause-and-effect relationships, or leaders who contributed changes in thinking. Again, your questions will help you organize the material you need to satisfy your interest and curiosity.

EXERCISE 35

1. What do you want to learn from this reference book?

2. **Survey** the book, using as many of the Ten Commandments as you can. In a reference, you will undoubtedly spend more time reading the contents and index, looking for organizational clues such as introductions and summaries, and evaluating the publication date as it relates to your needs.

   Survey:
   Title: _____
   Author or source: _____
   Publication date: _____
   Index: _____
   _____
   Preface, foreword, or introduction: _____
   _____
   _____
   Contents: _____
   _____
   Maps, graphs, illustrations, etc.: _____
   _____
   _____
   Reading difficulty: _____
   Summarize what you've learned: _____
   _____
   _____
   _____

3. Determine your specific **purpose** questions. Use the Question Ball for guidance.

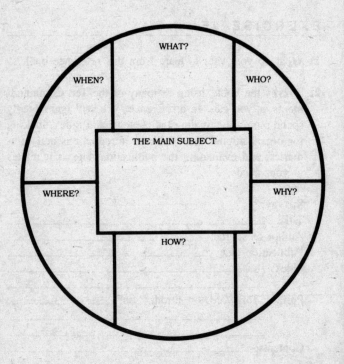

Write your **purpose** questions in order of importance in achieving your purpose.

_____
_____
_____
_____
_____
_____

4. Speculate the answers to your questions:

_____
_____
_____
_____
_____
_____

5. Read to find answers to your **purpose** questions. Jot down any notes you consider helpful.

_____
_____
_____
_____
_____
_____

6. Organize your thoughts and summarize your learning in outline form.

_____
_____
_____
_____
_____
_____

If you are not satisfied with what you have learned, establish new purpose questions and repeat the pattern.

EXERCISE 36

1. What do you want to learn from this biography or
   autobiography? _____
   _____
   _____

2. **Survey** the book, using as many of the Ten Commandments as you can. In a biography, you will want to spend
   time with any introduction or foreword, contents, index,
   and summaries on the book cover.

   Survey:
   Title: _____
   Author or source: _____
   Publication date: _____
   Index: _____
   _____

   Preface, foreword, or introduction: _____
   _____
   _____

   Contents: _____
   _____

   Maps, graphs, illustrations, etc.: _____
   _____
   _____

   Reading difficulty: _____
   Summarize what you've learned: _____
   _____
   _____
   _____

3. Determine your specific **purpose** questions. Use the
   Question Ball for guidance.

Write your **purpose** questions in order of importance in achieving your purpose.

_____
_____
_____
_____
_____
_____

4. Speculate the answers to your questions:

_____
_____
_____
_____
_____

5. Read to find answers to your **purpose** questions. Jot down any notes you consider helpful.

_____
_____
_____
_____
_____

6. Organize your thoughts and summarize your learning in outline form.

_____
_____
_____
_____
_____
_____

If you are not satisfied with what you have learned, establish new purpose questions and repeat the pattern.

EXERCISE 37

1. What do you want to learn from this book of philosophy?

_____

_____

_____

2. **Survey** the book, using as many of the Ten Commandments as you can. In a philosophy book, you will want to spend time with the contents, index, introduction or foreword, summaries on the cover, and background of the writer.

   Survey:
   Title: _____

   Author or source: _____

   Publication date: _____

   Index: _____

   _____

   Preface, foreword, or introduction: _____

   _____

   _____

   Contents: _____

   _____

   Maps, graphs, illustrations, etc.: _____

   _____

   Reading difficulty: _____

   Summarize what you've learned: _____

   _____

   _____

   _____

3. Determine your specific **purpose** questions. Use the Question Ball for guidance.

Write your **purpose** questions in order of importance in achieving your purpose.

_____
_____
_____
_____
_____
_____

4. **Speculate** the answers to your questions:

_____
_____
_____
_____
_____
_____

5. Read to find answers to your **purpose** questions. Jot down any notes you consider helpful.

_____
_____
_____
_____
_____
_____

6. Organize your thoughts and summarize your learning in outline form.

_____
_____
_____
_____
_____
_____

If you are not satisfied with what you have learned, establish new purpose questions and repeat the pattern.

Reading-Learning Flow Chart

The Learning Pattern—Cycle of Effective Learning Through Reading
The procedure through which you learn and apply your own knowledge to solve problems.

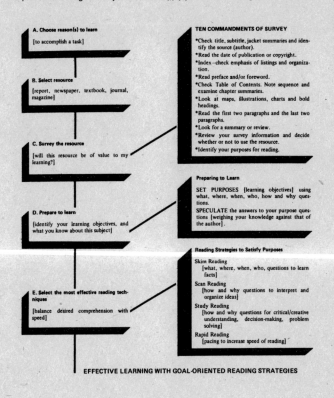

A. Choose reason(s) to learn

[to accomplish a task]

B. Select resource

[report, newspaper, textbook, journal, magazine]

C. Survey the resource

[will this resource be of value to my learning?]

D. Prepare to learn

[identify your learning objectives, and what you know about this subject]

E. Select the most effective reading techniques

[balance desired comprehension with speed]

TEN COMMANDMENTS OF SURVEY

* Check title, subtitle, jacket summaries and identify the source (author).
* Read the date of publication or copyright.
* Index—check emphasis of listings and organization.
* Read preface and/or foreword.
* Check Table of Contents. Note sequence and examine chapter summaries.
* Look at maps, illustrations, charts and bold headings.
* Read the first two paragraphs and the last two paragraphs.
* Look for a summary or review.
* Review your survey information and decide whether or not to use the resource.
* Identify your purposes for reading.

Preparing to Learn

SET PURPOSES [learning objectives] using what, where, when, who, how and why questions.

SPECULATE the answers to your purpose questions [weighing your knowledge against that of the author].

Reading Strategies to Satisfy Purposes

Skim Reading
 [what, where, when, who, questions to learn facts]

Scan Reading
 [how and why questions to interpret and organize ideas]

Study Reading
 [how and why questions for critical/creative understanding, decision-making, problem solving]

Rapid Reading
 [pacing to increase speed of reading]

EFFECTIVE LEARNING WITH GOAL-ORIENTED READING STRATEGIES

Evaluation Profile of Reading Habits

You've done it! You've completed the difficult challenge of changing your long-established habit of reading every word in any message to an efficient method of taking charge of what you receive and remember from those messages. Your skills will continue to improve as you practice them every time you read. You will be rewarded with a lifetime of well-managed reading time!

To evaluate how much you have grown in reading efficiency, turn back to the "Profile of Reading Habits" on page 4. This time place an *O* in the column that describes your present reading habits. Notice the changes from the *X* you placed on the profile before you began *Super Reading*.

You now possess the key to open all written knowledge—and fun. *Enjoy reading!*

Answers to Exercises

Answers for Exercises 1 through 6 are given after each article. The answers provided here are *suggested* answers, answers that use the skills of the program. Yours may not agree, but that's not important. What *is* important is your understanding the thinking process to apply when reading to obtain your answers.

EXERCISE 7

Safety and stock-car drivers.
You note the number of times the word *safety* and the number of times *stock-car drivers* or *drivers* appears in the article. Logically, you decide the discussion is of safety and stock-car drivers.

EXERCISE 8

Town of Regina Coeli in the Sabine Hills in Italy. Any or all three locations can be the correct answer depending on the detail you seek to achieve your purpose.

EXERCISE 9

When food is sucked into the windpipe.
Reading the beginning of the first sentence of each paragraph makes it clear that they all discuss treatment rather than causes until you see, "Choking occurs when . . ."

EXERCISE 10

Harald the Fair-Hair.
Reading beginnings of paragraphs finds the answer in paragraph 3.

EXERCISE 11

To conclude a treaty with Japan.
No helpful paragraph divisions, but reading the beginning of sentences is rapid.

EXERCISE 12

What?	*Flag of New Zealand.*
Who?	*No one is mentioned.*
When?	*New Zealand Day, Anzac Day, Queen Elizabeth's birthdays, opening of Parliament, and anniversary of each province.*
Where?	*On shore and on government vessels.*
How?	*With the Union Jack of Great Britain in the top left corner and the Southern Cross on a blue background.*
Why?	*New Zealand is part of Great Britain; the Southern Cross is a constellation visible there, used to indicate time and direction.*

EXERCISE 13

What?	*Tests of sensitivity to penicillin.*
Who?	*Dr. Frank Perlman.*
When?	*Not given.*
Where?	*At University of Oregon Medical School.*
How?	*Scratch test.*
Why?	*To see if tests are as perfect as they are thought to be.*

EXERCISE 14

1. *A. M. Sullivan.*
2. *Near Hackettstown, N.J.*

EXERCISE 15

1. *Icarus was character in Greek mythology. Arthur Clarke is scientist/science fiction writer.*
   Last paragraph, "... as a scientist who also wrote science fiction ... was the forerunner of men like Dr. Arthur Clarke. ..."
2. *Science fiction: Icarus for flight with wax wings, Dr. Clarke as "popularizer of space."*

EXERCISE 16

1. *Case Study.* First you have to determine which number is high and which is low. A lower number is "better" when 1 is high.
2. *Goals are across. Methods are down.*

EXERCISE 17

1. *Penicillin reaction.*
2. *Two extra days.*
3. *Bacteria may die before planted or finding bacteria may not indicate that it caused sore throat.*

EXERCISE 18

1. *A white comedian who originated Jim Crow Musical.*
2. *Minstrelsy ("Cullard Opera"). You'd begin by looking for the dates.*
3. *White performers took the rudiments of Williams' act and stylized them into successful formulas.*

EXERCISE 19

Some factors send them up, some down. You'd have to skim each paragraph to see the effect of the various long-range factors.

EXERCISE 20

1. Depending upon the amount of detail you need to satisfy your purpose, your answer could be simply: *He sowed the seeds of his own destruction, and a combination of several factors caused the fall.*

   If you needed more details, you could list at least 8 factors including, *horizontal integration was not effective; he was not creative; he failed to develop future management; his son did not possess leadership qualities; 16th Amendment, Physical Valuation Act, Federal Trade Commission Act, and Clayton Antitrust Act all limited power; public turned on Morgan as scapegoat; and it was the end of an era.*

2. *Most powerful of six key dispensers of credit.*

EXERCISE 21

The principles are listed and numbered.
Have a definite plan.
Don't overtrade.
Limit losses and allow profits to run.
Learn all you can about the commodity being traded.

EXERCISE 22

1. Read the bold headlines. Under **The Metric System**, skim-read to find a date followed by an explanation.
   The National Assembly of France requested the French Academy of Sciences to develop an invariable standard. Length was a portion of the earth's surface, and larger and smaller versions of each unit were created by multiplying or dividing by 10.
2. Skim-read to find *metron*.
   Greek "metron" meant "a measure."

EXERCISE 23

1. Skim-read for "harvest" and "weather."
   Must be totally dry for a day or two before they are harrowed.
2. Skim-read for "concentrations" or place names.
   Climate and geography is conducive to growth.
   You can continue with details of climate and geography if your purpose requires more specific details.
3. Use the headings.
   New lawns; gardens; shrubs and trees; roses; indoor gardens, potted plants, hanging baskets; mulching.

EXERCISE 24

1. The answers to these questions depend upon personal information: citizenship, country of entry, type of vehicle, licensed activities desired, pets, etc. Skim-read to find areas that pertain to you and your needs.
2. This is a personal opinion.

EXERCISE 25

1. Skim for word "cannibalism." Scan any paragraphs that discuss it.
   skull cap.
2. This necessitates putting facts read with your analysis of them.
   Utensils were buried with the dead for use in after-life, indicating religious belief in life after death.

EXERCISE 26

1. Your opinion might include *expanding coalmining and agriculture, forest fires, hunters. Solutions include zoos like Ragutan and rehabilitation centres like the one in Borneo.*
2. This would, of course, be a personal preference.

EXERCISE 27

1. This is a personal interpretation, but the author's statement about fighting "abuse" by "exposing" it may be useful.
2. This is completely personal.

EXERCISE 28

1. Scanning can provide an overview of what subjects are covered. Then the publication source may help you speculate.
2. Probably reading in more detail is necessary to arrive at an answer. You may want to divide such a broad topic into segments—politics, employment, education, etc.

EXERCISE 29

Answers are discussed after the **survey.**

EXERCISE 30

These answers would be based on your purposes for reading. Completion of your survey always leads to establishing *purpose* questions.

EXERCISE 31

1. *Water-Supply Sources for the Farmstead and Rural Home.*
2. *Farmer's Bulletin, U.S. Department of Agriculture.*
3. *Water Requirements, Ground Water Sources.*
4-7. Your answers.

EXERCISE 32

In surveying a series of articles—whether in a research report, magazine, professional journal, or a digest of other publications—you must pay particular attention to dates and sources of information. Try to establish the purpose of the publication: to present a variety of aspects of one subject (aluminum), a variety of subjects all related to a time or event (Civil War), subjects of interest to a particular segment of the population (engineers), etc. You may find that this insight into the focus by the publisher either eliminates your reading any further or heightens your interest.

The next step is to decide which portions (articles, chapters, subjects) interest you. There's no law requiring you to read from first to last word in any article or to read every article. Surveying becomes your yardstick of how much to read.

After these decisions, you're ready to continue the effective reading process of setting specific questions you want answered, speculating, and reading flexibly to find answers you seek.

By the year 2000, 2 out of 3 Americans could be illiterate.

It's true.

Today, 75 million adults… about one American in three, can't read adequately. And by the year 2000, U.S. News & World Report envisions an America with a literacy rate of only 30%.

Before that America comes to be, you can stop it… by joining the fight against illiteracy today.

Call the Coalition for Literacy at toll-free **1-800-228-8813** and volunteer.

Volunteer Against Illiteracy. The only degree you need is a degree of caring.

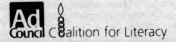

Ad Council Coalition for Literacy